Testimonials

Praise for the 2007 Edition of *Making 36%* and *Terry's Tips* (the option newsletter that carries out the 10K Strategy and its 36% Solution variation).

I would like to express my satisfaction with following: the 10K strategies on DIA, IWM, 36% Solution – Calls, 36% Solution – Puts, Big Bear and Russell 1, and SPY. I began the year with approximately $80K and thus far (December 3, 2007) I have just over $150K gross (before commissions). That represents about 87% growth. I did not have all these strategies in place from the beginning of the year, but I calculate that if I did, I could have well broken the century mark in growth percentage. This performance far surpasses anything I've ever done in stocks, mutual funds and (don't remind me), investment real estate. I'm definitely planning to increase my capital allocation for 2008. I also thank you for your recommendation of *thinkorswim*. They are a first rate outfit.

— BRAD DUNN

After 40 years of searching for the ideal strategy for a small investor, I'm so glad I found you. My Saturday mornings are spent eagerly awaiting your weekly report. Your 10K Strategy, as applied to IWM and EEM are near perfection for extremely good returns and manageable risk.

— WAYNE WOLF, CPA

I have been a subscriber to *Terry's Tips* for almost a year. This is a unique service which includes a once-a-week commentary on how the various portfolios are doing. This is an honest commentary unlike most services which try to cover their failings with [illegible] numbers. Terry actually discusses failures as well as successes. I [illegible] others are many more successes than failures. I ha[illegible]ng and can honestly say that I have lea[illegible]nd teaching than all of the books.

— JIM NEEDHAM

I love your program, and have been trading it for just over a year now. I also want to thank you for my new BMW 5 series. I promised myself, (and convinced my wife) that I would buy it once I doubled my initial investment through using your program. Between June, 2006 and October, 2007, I did it, and my new car is now on order.

— JOE P.

I was a subscriber back in the rough times we had trading back in 2004. I came back on board about 4 months ago and I have already made back 75% of what was lost back in 2004 in a full year's trading. I'm extremely glad I made the decision to come back.

— TOM LA BISSONIERE

I have been a subscriber of *Terry's Tips* for the past 5 months. Everyone should try his initial offer and get a feel for his service, web site and study the results. The service has been everything the site advertises. *Terry's Tips* service has exceeded all my expectations. He offers a very good service and speaking for my results, he has over-delivered.

— TOM STIDHAM

At 55 years old, I've been "playing" with the stock market for years, mostly with very limited success. The majority of my life savings is in multiple mutual funds which, as we all know, are considered superior if they (inconsistently) have returns of 10–11%. After less than six months of investing some IRA funds into two *Terry's Tips* portfolios (36% Solution, Puts and Smiling Spider), however, you've caused me to believe that I really will be able to retire on a nice income — and, hopefully, in the not too distant future. Thanks for the spectacular returns and thanks for being willing to share your knowledge and insights.

— CLIFF FRISH

Those who like to use the cliché that if it's too good to be true, it probably is, surely don't know about *Terry's Tips* and the 36% Solution! Being retired, I very much appreciate the concept of a monthly income generator that the 36% Solution has proven to be. Thanks for a little book that changed my life's perspective. I look forward to reading the new 2008 edition of *Making 36%* if for no other reason other than to savor the contented feeling I'll receive by reviewing what I was lucky enough to understand, appreciate, and benefit from when I read the first edition a year ago.

— Stanley E. Cassel, D.V.M.

I can't figure out why everyone isn't using calendar spreads using your method. Sometimes it seems too good to be true. My returns the past two years have been almost unbelievable. I don't even try to tell anyone about it because they wouldn't believe me.

— Fred R.

After 25+ years at this, I have seen a lot of experts come and go. I have only found two where I consistently make money by following their experience and methods; one that I have followed since the 80s in the Hogs and Bellies at the Chicago Merc, and you. Nice work!

— Bob DuPre

…. with the market at its current lower level, that in the past it would take months and some times years to recover with stocks and mutual funds, whereas the spreads that I have using your system take a couple of weeks to recover with far less upward movement in the market. I know that with my holdings in stocks and mutual funds in the past that the most recent decline would look pretty bad on my statements. Right now, I'm way ahead of my July holdings from the market peak over 14,000. I've pulled out $25,000 to remodel my house and I'm still $50,000 up in my account after the withdrawals.

— Marc Parker

I autotrade in 2 different accounts, all your strategies. I read everything you write on Saturdays. I love your happiness thoughts and everything else. I usually do not communicate at all but I had to tell you how well my accounts with you are doing compared to everything else. You are awesome. Keep up the good work.

— Maya Jagasia

I have made close to 8% a month since you started the 36% portfolio.

— Sanjeev

I don't know if a lot of subscribers thank you but my wife and I have watched the money that we have invested in your program grow at an alarming rate. We especially like the fact, which no other investments offer, the ability to cash out profits every month if they are earned. Cheers to you and your staff.

— ROB SLAVING

I have confidence in your system...I have seen it work very well...currently I have had a first 100% gain, and am now working to diversify into more portfolios. This kind of trading is actually an "art"... I have my own field of expertise...but sadly I can only offer my great appreciation to what you do so instinctively.

— JAY GIALLOMBARDO

I started with your service about 7 months ago using three different portfolios worth $70k. Those changed of course over time, but today I am using 5 of the portfolios and the value just crossed the $100k mark (actually $101k) this morning. I consider this quite remarkable considering I have been investing for the last 25 years and have never seen consistent gains as you have shown me.

— MARK BAILEY

I have a PhD in math, but make my living from computers (software). It is fair to say that during the last 25+ years I spent THOUSANDS of hours reading, learning, simulating and developing trading systems. Since I subscribed to your service, I spend most of my research time on it and I gain bigger and bigger confidence that "this is it" (for me). I learn something new from every single report. It is extremely useful for me that you don't simply list the changes to be made, but reveal the thought process behind them and discuss alternatives. I feel that these lessons will make me a better trader.

— JOSEPH J.

Just wanted to keep you informed of what I am doing in OIH. My profits to date are $18,322 (in 7 months) on a $34K investment using the 10K Strategy.

— ROGER ADAMS

I am very very pleased with the performance of the portfolios. I've been interested in options for a very long time, but this seems to work more of the time and with better results. So I just keep moving more and more money from my self directed Ameritrade account to the autotrade accounts at *thinkorswim*.

— Justin Woddis

I am fascinated Terry's philosophy and technique. After having suffered through several booms and many more busts with my modest, self-manage brokerage account, it's a true pleasure to be able to be invested in a vehicle that's not so directly tied to the fortunes of a single company. And while I could probably achieve this same ease-of-mind with a mutual or index fund, I would have to be happy with a far more modest gain than what I've experienced with Terry.

— Eugene Hill

I thought you might appreciate some kind words from a devoted follower of your 10K Strategy far across the Atlantic in Germany. Even though the markets have been a little bit choppy due to subprime issues and wild volatility, you continue to make money for me beyond my wildest expectations. I can only thank you for being there for me and turning my investment world into a new and rewarding experience.

As a side note, I have to admit that I have in the past spent a lot of money and time being tutored on trading options. None of these courses came close to explaining how to manipulate and adjust the given strategy as you have so expertly done in your 10K strategy literature. What I liked about your approach is that you've managed to explain your strategy in terms that the layman can understand.

— Phil Davis

Am I satisfied with *Terry's Tips* ? — YES, YES, YES. In June of this year, 2007, I started trading following *Terry's Tips*. I'm retired so I have the time to do my own trading and I enjoy trading. When the email notices arrive I always try to get a better price — sometimes I do and sometimes I don't. The reason for doing the trades is easy to understand, the trades are easy to do and best of all, it's profitable. Who could ask for more?

— Linda Nelson

After 47 years of being very active in the market, I feel as though we found the Holy Grail. Also, I can't tell you how happy I am with Kurt at *thinkorswim*. He has been most helpful and a delight to work with.

— PETER J. KUEHN

My portfolio had incurred many losses until I adopted Terry's strategies. (Two other investment newsletters) consistently lost money trading options (by betting on a positive or negative direction for the underlying). The Dr's strategy is the only one I have seen or tested myself that consistently produces profits, not the "hit it out of the park" profits that so many newsletter authors and advisors claim, but market beating profits that you can count on.

— TOMMY HIETT

I want to take some time to personally thank you. Not only thanks to you the money that I am investing is growing five times faster than before, but I have also spurred me to get informed, and I have learned a lot. I am actually finding myself able to understand and predict more and more what you will be telling us in next report.

The clarity of your explanations and the no-nonsense approach you take resonated really well with my engineering background. I loved how you talked numbers without hiding behind the lingo or the empty words. The track of record of your portfolios speaks a million words. I dare any mutual fund to beat that.

— ALESSANDRO CATORCINI

To see dozens of other testimonials about *Terry's Tips* and the *36% Solution*, go to www.TerrysTips.com/Testimonials.

MAKING 36%

*Duffer's Guide to Breaking Par
in the Market Every Year
in Good Years and Bad*

A Stock Options Strategy That Can
Be Mastered in One Round of Golf
(if Your Partner is Driving the Cart)

Dr. Terry F. Allen

Fuller Mountain Press
256 Fuller Mountain Road
Ferrisburgh, VT 05456

Printed in the United States

Library of Congress Control Number: 2006937199

ISBN – 9780-9776372-4-9

Although the author has extensively researched appropriate sources to ensure the accuracy and completeness of the information contained in this publication, the author and the publisher assume no responsibility for errors, inaccuracies, omissions, or any inconsistency herein.

This publication is designed to provide accurate and authoritative information in regard to the subject matter covered. It is sold with the understanding that neither the author nor the publisher is engaged in rendering legal, tax, accounting, investment, or other professional services. No such advice is intended or implied. Neither the author nor the publisher is a registered investment advisor.

Options involve risk and are not suitable for all investors. Option trading involves substantial risk. You can lose money trading options. All investors who deal with options should read and understand "Characteristics and Risks of Standardized Options." A free copy of this publication can be obtained from The Options Clearing Corporation, One North Wacker Drive, Suite 500, Chicago IL 60606. 312-322-6200.

All securities named in this publication have been included purely for purposes of illustration. No recommendations to buy, sell, or hold such securities, or any securities, is intended. Readers should use their own judgment. If advice or other expert assistance is required, the services of a competent professional should be sought.

This book is dedicated to my wife, Debbie,
the love of my life and my best friend,
who taught me that bookstores
are not the best place to sell books.

Second, this book is dedicated to
all of us who were born to golf,
but forced to work.

1

The man who takes up golf
to get his mind off his work
soon takes up work to
get his mind off golf.

Contents

Introduction 1

The Front Nine

1. Flat Markets Ahead 9
2. Don't Buy Individual Stocks 13
3. Don't Buy Mutual Funds 17
4. Winning the Loser's Game 21
5. Something to Think About 25
6. Pity Your Broker 27
7. Ignore the Analysts 31
8. About the Author 35
9. Options are Less Risky Than Stock 39

The Back Nine

10. Puts and Calls 101 49
11. Decay Chart of a Typical Option 55
12. Writing Calls Doesn't Work 61
13. Find the Right Underlying 65
14. Setting Up the 36% Solution 69
15. Making Adjustments 77
16. Trading Options in Your IRA 87
17. Find the Best Discount Broker 89
18. Summary of the 36% Solution 95

The 19th Hole, or When it is Raining or Dark

19. How to Get Started 103

Appendix A – Greeks and Implied Volatility 109
Appendix B – Why Puts Are Better Than Calls for Calendar Spreads .. 119
Appendix C – A Note on Early Exercise of Short Options 125
Appendix D – More About the Russell 2000 131
Appendix E – The Terry's Tips Track Record 137

Index 145

It is difficult to make predictions,
especially when they involve the future.

Introduction

This book is a little about golf and a lot about investing. For many years, I have been dismayed at the dismal returns most people made with their conventional investments. I knew from my 30 years of stock options experience that better returns were possible. I felt confident that I had developed a strategy that could make 36% a year in good years and bad.

I hope to reach a larger audience with this book by connecting it to golf. I know how much people love the sport. I understand that the picture of the golfer on the cover is like the thousands of advertisements we see that feature beautiful (often semi-clad) women to attract attention to un-sexy and mundane products. It must work, however, since they keep doing it.

So I must start out this book with an apology. I'm sorry that I am pandering to your love of golf to deliver my message about making exceptional investment returns on your money. I am an unabashed marketer, and I should be ashamed of myself.

I feel doubly responsible to deliver you some valuable information that can truly change your investment returns for the rest of your life. That is my challenge and fondest wish.

A couple of years ago, I started an Internet newsletter to teach people about stock options and the investment strategy I had developed over many years of trading options. I called it **www.TerrysTips.com.** Most of my early subscribers were attracted to a strategy that could make over 100% a year. At first, they were not disappointed.

I set up an actual account at the beginning of 2003 for my subscribers to follow. I sent them every trade as I placed it so they could mirror it if they wished. At the end of the year, I had exceeded the original goal by a long shot, and earned almost 200% for myself and the subscribers who mirrored my trades.

In 2005, I set up eight actual portfolios with different underlying stocks for my subscribers to follow. Some of the portfolios had

1

God does not charge time spent golfing
against a man's allotted life span.

— GOLFER'S CREED

lower profit goals and lower risk profiles as well, such as one based on the Dow Jones Industrial Average which sought 20% to 30% a year (it earned 52% in its first two years of existence while the Dow rose about 5%). While this "conservative" portfolio dragged down the average of the other portfolios, **the average annualized gain (after commissions) for all eight portfolios was 103% for 2005** (of course, past performance does not guarantee future results). 2006 was also a successful year. The average gain for 11 actual portfolios was over 50% (after commissions) for the year.

So now you are wondering about 2004. That was a learning year. The strategy I had employed so successfully up to 2003 completely fell apart when option prices fell to nine-year lows and the market became quite choppy. I made some big changes in the strategy to handle the new market conditions, and I like to think that the results in 2005, 2006, and 2007 proved that the changes made the difference.

In February 2007, I set up the *36% Solution* whose basic principles were the same as the higher-risk portfolios of earlier years but the annual profit goal was 36% with an extremely high likelihood of achieving it. This book is all about the *36% Solution*.

In 2001, John Wiley published an earlier book I wrote — *No Cash, No Fear: Entrepreneur's Guide to Starting Any Business Without Money*. I was disappointed with the way the book was marketed. I decided I would market the next book I wrote on my own.

In *No Cash, No Fear* (which is largely auto-biographical), I discouraged readers from investing in stock options. Without a well-thought-out and tested strategy like the *36% Solution*, I was well aware of how easy it was to lose big money with stock options. I knew that an options strategy had to be the subject of a second book. And here it is, at last.

When my wife, Debbie Allen, decided to write a book about tending perennial gardens, I encouraged her to self-publish rather than depend on a traditional publisher to market the book. (It is called *Garden Notes From Muddy Creek: A Twelve-Month Guide to Tending Ornamental Perennials.*)

1

Golf was once a rich man's sport,
but now it has millions of poor players.

The book was good enough to be adopted by a national distributor which placed it in bookstores throughout the country. One day she visited the local Border's store where only a single copy had been sold and then stopped at a coffee shop which had sold a hundred copies.

She came home and exclaimed "Book stores are a lousy place to sell books." Her observation set off a light bulb in my head. My idea was to use golf pro shops as my outlet, and write something that might have appeal to golfers as well as investors. Who knows, maybe some people are both golfers and investors?

Publishing a book myself has some downsides, however. I have been totally discounted by the financial press because I have the audacity to claim possible returns that are far above what "everyone" knows is possible. I sent review copies of my book to every major financial publication (and as many minor ones as I could find) and *not one single publication would write a review*. Apparently, no one wants to take the risk that I would ultimately turn out to be a charlatan, and they would be discredited somewhere down the line.

The biggest difficulty I have had in selling this book is my credibility. I have simply promised too much. It doesn't seem to matter much that I have actually achieved these gains, and much more, for several years. Both for myself and my *Terry's Tips* subscribers.

Imagine the credibility problem I would have if I had called the book "Making 50%" or "Making 60%," even though those returns are more typical of how this strategy has performed over the last three years.

Now that you have found this book, I feel a tremendous responsibility to not disappoint you. If you have any questions about options, I will try to answer them; email me at **Terry@TerrysTips.com**. I am not a licensed investment advisor, so I can't offer you advice on your personal investments, but I can answer most questions concerning options. I hope you enjoy reading this book as much as I enjoyed writing it. I look forward to prospering with you.

1
The
FRONT
NINE
(Foreplay)

1

A golf match is a test of your skill
against your opponent's luck.

HOLE 1
Flat Markets Ahead

Thomas Friedman, in *The World is Flat*,[1] explained how the entire world has become flat, and why it will continue to become flatter in the future. He could have said the same thing about stock markets.

Some of the smartest people in the world see flat markets ahead. Warren Buffet, America's most successful investor, writing in 2004, said that he expects at least 10 years of flat markets.[2]

In 2006, Robert Arnott said "15 years from now, stock prices won't be materially higher than they are today."[3]

Value Line predicts three to five years of flat markets (starting in 2004).[4] One of the most accurate of all long-term market-timing models is the one based on projections from analysts at *Value Line* for price changes over the next three to five years for the 1,700+ stocks they monitor. While their short-term forecasts have not been particularly accurate, their longer-term predictions have been remarkably on the money for over 30 years.

The *Value Line* three to five year projections are extremely valuable for many reasons:

1) Their analysts are independent and immune from the pressures that can be found in research departments associated with investment banks and brokerage firms.
2) Few other firms besides *Value Line* even bother to focus on what will happen in three to five years, concentrating instead on just the next 12 months.
3) The large number of stocks they cover means that random errors in individual stocks become insignificant. (The indicator is the median projection of almost 2000 separate forecasts). Analyst errors on individual stocks tend to cancel each other out.

When *Value Line* predicts lower or flat markets in three to five years, we all should take notice.

*When I die, bury me on the golf course
so my husband will visit.*

— AUTHOR UNKNOWN

Some observers see a slightly better scenario than a flat market. Jack Bogle, founder of Vanguard and one of the most respected professionals in the financial world, expects that market returns will decline to an average of 7% in coming decades. Even this rosy scenario pales in comparison to the historic averages we have enjoyed for the past few decades.

So let's face it. Markets are likely to be flat, or at best, moderately higher for the next several years. How will you cope with this new reality? Where will you put your money? One thing is certain — what has worked in the past will surely not work in the future. You can't just buy the market and hope prices will go up.

In this little book, I will explain an options strategy where maximum gains come in flat markets. In fact, I will prove mathematically that if the market stays absolutely flat, the strategy will make over 100% a year. Then I will show how it can dependably make 36% every year even when the market fluctuates up and down as we all know it is likely to do.

1. Thomas L Friedman, *The World is Flat: A Brief History of the Twenty-First Century* (New York: Farrar, Straus and Giroux, 2005)
2. Quoted by Rich Karlgaard, *Forbes,* October 4, 2004.
3. Robert D. Arnott, chairman of Research Affiliates (*New York Times,* October 1, 2006 article by Paul J. Lim).
4. Mark Hulbert, *New York Times,* July 18, 2004.

1

Individuals should not be buying individual stocks.
They should assume that the information and advice
they receive regarding individual stocks are stale and,
to a large degree, already incorporated in stock prices.

— Dan Reingold,
Confessions of a Wall Street Analyst

You don't own stocks. Stocks own you.

— Tony Balis,
Founder, www.humanity.org

HOLE 2
Don't Buy Individual Stocks

Some reasons why a stock price might fall:

• An analyst down-grades the stock.
• The company fails to meet expected quarterly earnings.
• The company achieves expected earnings but fails to meet the "whisper" numbers.
• The company meets the "whisper" earnings number but falls short of sales expectations.
• The company meets the "whisper" numbers but issues a gloomy outlook for the future.
• The company gets hit with a lawsuit.
• The company is accused of corporate shenanigans:
  – Cooking the books
  – Back-dating management stock options grants
  – Selling unsafe products (and knowing about them)
  – Patent infringement
  – Etc.
• The company loses a big contract to a competitor.
• The market as a whole falls, taking down most stocks with it.

If you own stock in an individual company, any of the above things (and many more) can happen to your stock at any time. And probably ruin your day.

When you own an individual stock, you are sitting on a financial time bomb.

On the other hand, if you own a broad-based Exchange Traded Fund (ETF) like the S&P 500 SPDRS or the Russell 2000 (small cap), you only have to worry about a general market decline. If this happens, you will be moaning along with everyone else.

No one likes a falling stock portfolio. But it is a whole lot less painful when everyone else is in the same boat.

*Did you ever notice that it's a lot
easier to get up at 6:00 a.m. to play golf
than at 10:00 to mow the lawn?*

The bottom line is that owning an individual stock is almost as bad an idea as buying a full-load mutual fund (see the next chapter). You might get lucky and make some money, but most of the time you will not beat the market averages.

If you insist on buying individual stocks regardless of the miserable odds of being successful, there is an options strategy that works better than the outright purchase of the stock. I call it the Shoot Strategy (as in shoot for the stars). If the stock goes up, the strategy will result in far greater percentage gains than if you had bought the stock instead. And if the stock stays flat, you will make a small profit — something you wouldn't make if you just owned the stock. While the Shoot Strategy is outside the purview of this book, you can read about it at **www.TerrysTips.com/Tip5.**

1

In my opinion, investing in a diversified portfolio
of mutual funds ranks among the worst possible investments.
The problem with funds is fees. The longer you invest
in a mutual fund, the more you pay in fees.

— ROBERT KIYOSAKI, CO-AUTHOR, *RICH DAD, POOR DAD*

Never Buy a Mutual Fund

Why would anyone put his or her hard-earned money into an investment that has a 75% chance of losing?

Charles Ellis in *Winning the Loser's Game* reports that — "The historical record is that on a cumulative basis, over three-quarters of professionally managed funds *under*performed the S&P 500 Stock Average...over the past 50 years, mutual funds have lost 180 basis points — compounded annually — compared to the S&P 500."

He continues, "Even more disconcerting... the average mutual fund investor gets a return that is significantly below the return of the average mutual fund. From 1984 to 1995 the investors' shortfall was a stunning 6% annually, almost one-half of the 12.3% 'earned' by the average equity mutual fund,... The reason: frequent trading or turnover. Instead of staying the course with their investments, many investors tried to time the market, holding a fund for less than three years before selling and buying something else." [1]

How would you make out if you only bought the highest-ranking mutual funds? *Morningstar* is the most respected source — each year they rank all the mutual funds from one-star (the worst) to five-stars (the best). If you purchased only five-star rated funds, you would find that in the following year, over 50% of those funds would underperform the S&P 500. Regression to the mean is a much more powerful likelihood than a continuation of the exceptional returns for the prior year. [2]

Jack Bogle is considered to be the father of the index fund industry. He is known as the man who left over $20 billion on the table when he set up the Vanguard Group as a "mutual" rather than taking it public or owning it outright himself (which he could have done). He criticizes the financial industry for "telling everyone that they can do better than average, even after paying fees and transactions costs to support the lavish incomes of brokers and fund managers." [3]

1

Golf is 90 percent mental
and 10 percent mental.

If mutual fund managers really can't outperform the market, why do we pay them so much? Year after year, millions of investors pay mutual fund managers billions of dollars to underperform the market. It's one of the investment world's strangest mysteries. Does it make sense to you?

Jack Bogle and Charley Ellis are not alone in recommending index funds —

- Warren Buffet said in his *Berkshire Hathaway Annual Report* in 1996, "Most investors...will find that the best way to own common stocks is through an index fund that charges minimal fees."
- "Most individual investors would be better off in an index mutual fund." — Peter Lynch
- "Most of my investments are in equity index funds." — William F. Sharpe, Nobel Laureate in Economics, 1990
- Even a famous stock broker agrees; "Most of the mutual fund investments I have are index funds, approximately 75%." — Charles R. Schwab

A $10,000 investment in 1982 in an index fund matching the S&P 500 grew to $109,000 by the end of 2002, while an identical investment in the average managed stock fund would have grown to $63,600. The reason: While the S&P 500 returned 12.7% a year, costs reduced the average stock fund's annual return to 9.7%.[4]

What further proof do you need that non-index mutual funds are one of the worst places to put your money? Yet I'll bet that most golfers own mutual funds.

As Charley Ellis points out, "Las Vegas is busy every day, so we know that not everyone is rational."

1. Charles D. Ellis, *Winning the Loser's Game*, McGraw-Hill, 2002.
2. Ibid
3. Weekend Interview with Jack Bogle, *Wall Street Journal,* September 2–3, 2006.
4. Ibid

1

The investor's chief problem — and even his worst enemy — is likely to be himself.

— BENJAMIN GRAHAM,
LEGENDARY INVESTOR AND WARREN BUFFET'S GURU

Golf is the only sport where your most feared opponent is you.

— ANON

HOLE 4
Winning the Loser's Game

D r. Simon Ramo, writing in *Extraordinary Tennis for the Ordinary Tennis Player,*[1] said that in professional tennis, about 80% of points resulted from winning shots, while in amateur tennis, about 80% of points were the result of one player making a mistake.

Professional tennis is a winner's game, while amateur tennis (and golf) is a loser's game.

My graduate school classmate, Charley Ellis, in his delightful and valuable investment guide, *Winning the Loser's Game,* extended Ramo's observation to the investment world: "Likewise, the 'money game' we call investment management has evolved in recent decades from a winner's game to a loser's game... In just 40 years the market activities of the investing institutions shifted from only 10% of total public transactions to an overwhelming 90%... No longer was the active investment manager competing with cautious custodians or amateurs who were out of touch with the market: Now he or she was competing with other experts in a loser's game where the secret to winning is to lose less than the others lose."[2]

Amateur golf is also a loser's game. As Tommy Armour said in his book *How to Play Your Best Golf All the Time* says: "The best way to win is by making fewer bad shots."[3] Rather than exerting supreme effort to hit the perfect golf shot, the amateur golfer is a whole lot better off working toward consistency and avoidance of bad shots.

In this little book, I will show you a simple system using options that will allow you to win the loser's game by increasing your odds of investment success. When you buy a stock, your odds of winning are a little better than 50% (since most stocks eventually go up).

Once you understand how the *36% Solution* works and put it to work, you considerably increase your odds of winning the loser's game. Not only will you make greater gains when the stock goes up, but you will also prosper if the stock stays absolutely flat, and you can also gain if the stock falls (as long as it doesn't fall too much).

1

Most golfers, like most businessmen,
swat the ball with all their might and
trust more or less to luck as to the result.

— B.C. FORBES,
FOUNDER, *FORBES* MAGAZINE

In this book, I acknowledge that I am asking you to take a great leap of faith. I have taken the position that the *36% Solution* has *less* risk than conventional stock and mutual fund investments, and at the same time, can be expected to generate profits which are two or three times greater than those "normal" investments. I understand that such a statement is contrary to the basic principle of investing that risk and reward are correlated — high-potential return means high risk, and low-potential return generally means a lower risk is taken.

I believe that you can win the loser's game while the professionals cannot. The big guys can't even play this game. They need to place hundreds of millions of dollars for their clients. There is not enough liquidity in the option markets for their purposes.

There is, however, sufficient liquidity in the option markets to invest $100,000 or more. I have had $2 million invested many times in option strategies similar to the *36% Solution* without incurring any problems with liquidity.

There seems to be a niche in the options market for winning the loser's game — a niche too small for the big guys but plenty big enough for you and me.

1. Simon Ramo, *Extraordinary Tennis for the Ordinary Tennis Player,* (New York: Crown Publishers, 1977).
2. Charles D. Ellis, *Winning the Loser's Game,* (New York: McGraw-Hill, 2002).
3. Tommy Armour, *How to Play Your Best Golf All the Time,* (New York: Simon & Schuster, 1971).

Don't play too much golf.
Two rounds a day are plenty.

— Harry Vardon

HOLE 5
Something to Think About

Have you ever thought about who is on the other side of any trade you make in the market?

Professional investors — financial institutions, mutual funds, investment banks, hedge funds, etc. — collectively account for about 90% of stock market volume.[1] These are the real professionals. They have more resources, more access to inside information, more money than you, and their decisions are made by the brightest, best-paid, full-time and highly-educated people that money can buy.

Every time you make a trade in the market, the chances are about nine out of ten that the other side of the transaction is taken by one of these smart professionals who has all the resources that you are lacking.

So if you are buying, they are selling. If you are selling, they are buying. Just think about that for a minute.

When you buy a stock, it is usually because you have just read an article or two about the company, or received a tip from a friend or broker. When a professional buys a stock, it is usually after extraordinary research, including talking with top management of the company (and top management of competitors), monitoring of supply chain and industry developments, attending trade association meetings, tracing inventory trends, consulting economists, industry specialists, securities analysts and other experts.

Just because the professionals do 20 times as much research as you do before making an investment decision doesn't mean they will always be right and you will be wrong. But who do you think has the better odds of being right?

You can easily select the absolute best car to buy, but if you pay too much, it really is not a good deal. The same is true for stocks, and the person who is selling you the stock knows a whole lot more about it than you do. Just think about that next time you buy or sell a stock.

1. Charles D. Ellis, *Winning the Loser's Game,* (New York: McGraw-Hill, 2002).

1

To my broker — even if he has,
from time to time, made me just that.

— ANDREW TOBIAS,
THE ONLY INVESTMENT GUIDE YOU WILL EVER NEED

Doctors bury their mistakes.
Brokers just take a second commission.

— UNKNOWN

HOLE 6
Pity Your Broker

The poor sucker just doesn't know. He is trying his best to make you happy and keep his job, but it is all a crap shoot. He knows all too well that he just doesn't know. And yet he is required to pretend that he does.

Sounds like an ulcer-producing job to me.

Remember that your broker does not make money *for* you — he makes it *from* you.

Your broker depends on his firm's analysts for investment ideas. Of course, the analysts are generally a bunch of lemmings who don't know either. If their ratings are consistent with most of the other analysts, they are playing it safe. They will probably keep their jobs.

Your broker loves it when you bring a stock to him. He can tell you that the stock is not on his firm's "Buy" list, but he secretly hopes you will buy it anyway so he makes a commission and it was your idea. You have let him (and his analysts) off the hook. He loves you. Good work!

Your broker will most certainly never tell you about trading options. Some reasons:

- He doesn't know anything about option trading (for years, I have been dismayed by the utter lack of understanding that most brokers have about options — no matter how educated or experienced they might be).
- Commission rates at full-service brokers are too high for you to make money trading options, especially the kind of spreads I recommend (each spread involves two commissions).
- Everyone "knows" that options are extremely risky. Since most options expire worthless, option traders must be losing their shirts. If he recommends options to you, and you lose money, you may sue him. He wants to keep his job.

1

Rise early. Work hard. Strike oil.

— J. Paul Getty

Sleep late. Play two rounds.
Use the 36% Solution.

— Terry Allen

Your broker is probably a really nice guy. He may even be your favorite golfing buddy. Don't embarrass him by showing him this book. He will tell you that it is a bunch of crap. If enough people start trading the *36% Solution* he will be out of a job. This book is a threat to his very existence.

1

The message (that attempting to beat the market is futile) can never be sold on Wall Street because it is in effect telling stock analysts to drop dead.

— PAUL SAMUELSON, NOBEL PRIZE LAUREATE

HOLE 7
Ignore the Analysts

If 20 out of 22 analysts rate XYZ a "buy" or a "strong buy," that is probably an excellent reason to *sell* the stock.

Most of those analysts' clients have already bought the stock. They did it when the analyst first made his or her recommendation. There may not be many people left to buy the stock.

On the other hand, if an analyst downgrades the stock, all hell breaks loose. If 20 out of 22 analysts have already put out a "buy" recommendation, the odds are ten to one that any change in their assessment will be on the downside. And downgrades kill a stock.

A couple of years ago, I searched for a stock that was likely to be a real dog. I wanted to find a company that had a very good chance of falling, or at least was very unlikely to go up. My goal was to set up an options strategy that would make 100% a year if the stock stayed flat (or fell by any amount). It is a relatively easy thing to do, actually, if the stock behaves as you expect, but that is another story.

I found a stock that almost every analyst just hated. In one magazine article, several analysts were asked to select their single best short sale candidate. Two of them selected this same company — Dillard Department Stores (DDS). One analyst explained that "Dillard can't compete with K-Mart or Wal-Mart on price, or get the margins of more upscale stores." While most analysts rank companies as *strong buy, buy,* or *hold* (which is generally a euphemism for *sell*), an amazing 70% of analysts rated DDS as *sell* or *strong sell*. I had never seen such a universal condemnation of a company like this.

Surely, Dillard was the dog of all dogs, just what I was looking for. Even its stock symbol reminded me of a root canal.

Over the next eight months, while the market in general *fell* by 8%, DDS *went up* by 50%. A year later, it was 100% higher than when the analysts picked it as their favorite short sale candidate. My option strategy using the stock also suffered until I bit the bullet and closed it down.

ﮊﮊ

1

There should be some professional exam for analysts.
Most of the time they talk through their backsides.

— ALAN SUGAR,
FOUNDER, AMSTRAD ELECTRONICS COMPANY

I learned my lesson. Next time I find a stock that is so universally hated by the experts, I am more likely to buy it than sell it. But as you know, I don't think that buying (or selling) stock in individual companies is a very good idea in any event. I far prefer an option strategy that makes money even if the underlying stock goes down.

There is only one success — to be able
to spend your life in your own way.

— Christopher Morley

About The Author

My name is Terry Allen. I am an options addict. I am old enough to collect Social Security, and I continue to trade options every day. I have traded options ever since they were "invented" in 1973. When I am not trading options, I am thinking about them. I even dream about options.

Along the way, I got an MBA from the Harvard Business School. A few years later I earned a Doctorate in Business Administration at the University of Virginia.

While at Virginia, I lived in the computer lab, trying out various option strategies. At the time, the publicly-traded options industry was just starting and option prices were quite inefficient. I created a computer model to help me make trading decisions. It was easy to make huge profits. I doubled my money every six months for two years while I was still a doctoral student.

Then I headed for Chicago. I leased a seat on the Chicago Board Options Exchange (CBOE) and traded on the floor. Then a couple of math professors named Black and Scholes developed and published a computer model that told everyone what option prices should be. Their model was very much like the one I had created. It killed my golden goose. To this day, the Black-Scholes model (or one similar to it) is used by nearly all professional option traders. Option prices are now quite efficient. It is a much greater challenge to make extraordinary profits. But it is still possible.

In many years, I doubled my money trading options, but the most important years were those when I lost money. Those were the times when I really learned something. In fact, I would be suspicious of any options "expert" who has never had a bad year. He probably hasn't been in the business long enough to appreciate the deeper risks of option trading.

My early success spoiled me. I believed that if I didn't make at least 100% every year, I was failing. It was not until recently that I altered

1

Half of golf is fun.
The other half is putting.

my strategy so that I could pursue a more reasonable annual profit goal and have an extremely high likelihood of achieving it.

Trading options has been good to me. In the late 1990s, I set a goal of giving away an average of $1000 every day for the rest of my life to worthy Vermont charities. I built a swimming pool for the Burlington Boys & Girls Club. I have provided several hundred thousands of dollars in college scholarships for low-income Vermonters and single parents. So far, I have given away over $2,000,000 to more than 50 Vermont charities.

In 2001, I created **www.TerrysTips.com**, an options investment newsletter, so that I could continue my charitable endeavors. I eventually ran more than ten actual option portfolios with differing underlying stocks and risk profiles so my subscribers could see how different strategies work over time.

In 2005, the SEC brought suit against me for providing personalized advice to subscribers without being a licensed investment advisor. They also objected to a statement on my website that they believed was misleading. While not admitting nor denying guilt, I paid a $230,000 fine and have continued my investment newsletter, now being careful not to provide individual personalized advice or make misleading statements.

So when I tell you that I have developed an options strategy that makes 36% every year, in good years and bad, I better be pretty sure that the statement is supported by strong evidence. I know the SEC is looking over my shoulder.

My goal in this book is to teach you that strategy without your having to become an options nut like me to carry it off. I wish us both luck.

1

Don't play for safety — it's the most
dangerous thing in the world.

— Hugh Walpole

HOLE 9

Options are Less Risky Than Stock

M ost people believe that option players are extreme risk takers. After all, they purchase an asset with a very short life, and hope it skyrockets in value. Option buyers might make 500% or more if they buy the right option, just as they would do if they picked the winning horse at the track.

The waiting period to see if you're a big winner is a little longer than a horse race, but not much. In a month or two, if the stock does not go the way you guessed, you lose your entire investment. Just tear up your ticket. You picked the wrong horse.

If the stock stays flat, most option buyers lose most or all of their bet as well. No wonder people think option trading is risky. At least if you buy a stock, and it stays flat, you don't lose anything but the opportunity to have done better with another investment.

When you buy an option, it is a declining asset. It depreciates faster than a new car. It becomes worthless in a matter of months.

High-risk, high-reward — that is an investment fact embraced by most people. They believe that any system that offers the opportunity for extraordinary profits must necessarily involve an inordinately high degree of risk.

Nothing could be further from the truth when it comes to intelligent options trading.

I am reminded of the ancient story of the blind men examining an elephant — each man touched a single part of the animal, and came to an entirely different conclusion as to what it was.

Viewed as single transactions, the following two statements are undeniably true:

1) Buying stock options is extremely risky.

Options decline in value every day the stock stays flat. Most options expire absolutely worthless, and the person who bought them loses his or her entire investment.

When you bet on a sure thing — hedge!

— Robert Half

2) Selling stock options is even more risky.

Selling stock options, when viewed as a single transaction, is even worse. Selling an option alone is called selling naked (because that's how you feel the whole time you have that position in your account). You have the theoretical possibility of unlimited loss. You can lose many times more money than you invested. At least at the horse race, you only lose the money you bet.

No wonder people believe that stock options investing is risky. There seems to be extreme risk all around. Just like the blind men examining the elephant, they are only looking at a single part of the picture.

Since most people have not taken the time to understand stock options, they too quickly conclude that the risk level is too high for them, and put their money into a "safe" place like mutual funds. Somehow if they are paying some "expert" to pick the stocks they own, they delude themselves into believing they are investing prudently.

To my way of thinking, nothing could be further from the truth.

Below is a graph of what profit or loss will accrue in five weeks at different stock price points with a typical $10,000 investment in the *36% Solution* (solid line) compared to the purchase of 100 shares of stock when the stock price is $72 (dotted line).

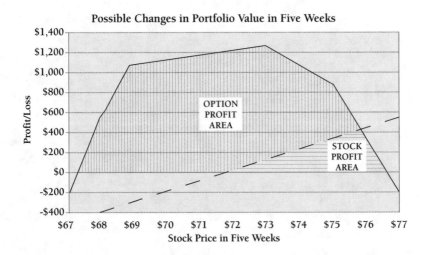

A regulation golf ball has 336 dimples.
I wonder who counted them.

This graph clearly shows that the only way for the stock investment to make money is for the stock to go up by a healthy amount. If the stock goes down, the investment loses $100 for every dollar it falls. If the stock goes down $3 in five weeks, the *36% Solution* still makes over 10% for the period while the stock investment loses 4%. If the stock goes up by $3, the stock investment gains 4% but the *36% Solution* gains more than double that amount. Which investment looks less risky to you?

If your money is in a mutual fund, even if it is an index fund, these are the facts:

1) If stocks go up, you will **make money** (but your profits will be reduced by the management fees, sales fees, and expenses you incur). For the past 50 years, the stock market has gained an average of about **10% a year**. That is the most gain you should expect with your mutual fund investments. We have already seen that the average mutual fund investor has historically made only 6.3% a year. Furthermore, as we discussed earlier, most prognosticators expect lower annual returns in the future .

2) If stocks stay flat, you **lose money** (management fees and inflation reduce the value of your holdings).

3) If stocks go down in value, you **lose even more money**.

Contrast those facts with the case of a properly executed stock options strategy (such as the *36% Solution*):

1) If the underlying stock goes up, you **make money**, often at a rate of over 36% a year.

2) If the underlying stock stays flat, you **make money**, often at a rate of over **100% a year**.

3) If the underlying stock goes down, you **may still make a profit**. Only if the stock goes down considerably in a very short time will you lose money. (Of course, your mutual fund would get clobbered in this scenario as well.)

⚑

*Reverse every natural instinct and do
the opposite of what you are inclined to do,
and you will probably come very close
to having a perfect golf swing.*

— BEN HOGAN

Which of the above two investments is the most risky? It seems to me that the mutual fund investment is a whole lot riskier than the stock options investment (not to mention that it yields a profit of only about one-sixth what the stock option portfolio might gain).

Why then does stock option investing get such a bad rap on the risk issue? People look at only a single part of the picture (buying or selling options) and ignore the total picture.

They conclude that if buying options is dangerous, and selling options is even more dangerous, then option trading must be doubly dangerous. **It does not occur to most people that a system of simultaneously buying and selling options might be even less risky than owning the stock.** This is the case, but most people never take the next step and learn the entire story.

The truth is that a properly-executed stock options strategy is considerably less risky than the purchase of stock or a mutual fund. However, it takes work. You will have to learn a little about how options work, and be an active part of the investment process. You can't plunk down your money like you do with a mutual fund and passively ignore your investment (although later in this book, I will show you how you can farm out the whole job to someone else).

The fact that stock options investing takes work discourages most people from even considering such an investment. That is fine with me. When I compare my returns each year with what the mutual funds are making, I feel like a real winner. I may work a little harder, but that's a small price to pay for the returns I make.

1

The

BACK
NINE

(Enjoy the game)

1

I don't want the cheese.
I just want to get out of the trap.

— SPANISH PROVERB

Puts and Calls 101

Here are the bare basic definitions of puts and calls. For a more complete discussion of stock options, please check out Appendix A. If you are already familiar with the basics of puts and calls, please feel free to skip over this chapter.

Basic Call Option Definition. Buying a *call option* gives you the right (but not the obligation) to purchase 100 shares of a company's stock at a certain price (called the strike price) from the date you buy the call until the third Friday of a specific month (called the expiration date).

People buy *calls* because they hope the stock will go up, and they will make a profit, either by selling the calls at a higher price, or by exercising their option (i.e., buying the shares at the strike price when the market price is higher).

Basic Put Option Definition. Buying a *put option* gives you the right (but not the obligation) to sell 100 shares of a company's stock at a certain price (called the strike price) from the date of purchase until the third Friday of a specific month (called the expiration date).

People buy *puts* because they hope the stock will go down, and they will make a profit, either by selling the puts at a higher price, or by exercising their option (i.e., forcing the seller of the put to buy the stock at the strike price at a time when the market price is lower).

LEAPS are long-term stock options. They have at least a year or two of life. LEAPS is an acronym for Long-term Equity AnticiPationS. All LEAPS expire in January.

Some Useful Details: Both put and call options are quoted in dollar terms (e.g., $3.50), but they actually cost 100 times the quoted amount (e.g., $350), plus an average of $1.50 commission (charged by my discount broker — commissions charged by other brokers may be considerably higher).

*The reason the pro tells you to keep your head down
is so you can't see him laughing.*

— PHYLLIS DILLER

Since most stock markets go up over time, and most people invest in stock because they hope prices will rise, there is more interest and activity in *call* options than there is in *put* options.

Real World Example of Call Options

Here are some call option prices for a hypothetical XYZ company on November 1, 2007 (price of stock: $45.00):

	Expiration Date			
Strike Price	**Nov '07**	**Dec '07**	**Jan '09**	**Terminology of Option**
		(price of call option)		
40	$5.50	$7.00	$18.50	"in-the-money" (strike price is less than stock price)
45	$2.00	$4.00	$16.00	"at-the-money" (strike price is equal to stock price)
50	$0.50	$1.00	$14.00	"out-of-the-money" (strike price is greater than stock price)

The *premium* is the price a call option buyer pays for the right to be able to buy 100 shares of a stock without actually having to shell out the money the stock would cost. The greater the time period of the option, the greater the premium.

The premium (same as the price) of an in-the-money call is composed of the *intrinsic value* and the *time premium*. (I understand that this is confusing. For in-the-money options, the option price, or premium, has a component part that is called the time premium). The intrinsic value is the difference between the stock price and the strike price. Any additional value in the option price is called the time premium. In the above example, the Dec '07 40 call is trading at $7.00. The intrinsic value is $5 ($45 stock price less 40 strike price), and the time premium is $2.

If you drink, don't drive. Don't even putt.

— DEAN MARTIN

For at-the-money and out-of-the-money calls, the entire option price is time premium. The greatest time premiums are found in at-the-money strike prices.

Call options are a way of leveraging your money. You are able to participate in any upward moves of a stock without having to put up all the money to buy the stock. However, if the stock does not go up in price, the option buyer may lose 100% of his/her investment. For this reason, buying options is considered by most people to be a risky investment.

As we will see soon, however, if you simultaneously buy and sell options, your resulting investment can be far less risky than owning stock or a mutual fund.

Golf gives you an insight into human nature,
your own as well as your opponent's.

— GRANTLAND RICE

HOLE 11

Decay Rate for a Typical Option

If the price of the stock remains the same, all options become less valuable over time. This makes total sense. If you own an option that has a year to go before it expires, you would be willing to pay more for it than you would for an option that lasted only a month.

The amount that the option falls in value is called its *decay*. There are two interesting aspects of decay. First, it tends to be quite low when there is a long time until the option expires. Second, decay increases dramatically as the option moves toward the date when it expires (the expiration date).

Below is a chart for a typical 12-month call option for a $70 stock. The strike price is $70 as well. If you were to buy this call option when it had 12 months until expiration, you would pay $7.80 ($780 per option). The stock would have to go up above $77.80 before you made a profit on the option if you held it until expiration.

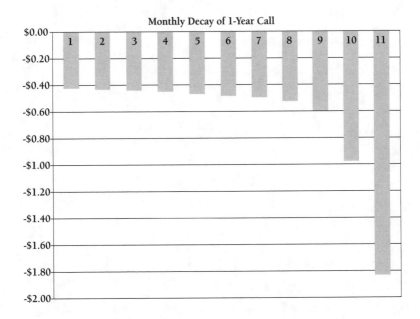

Monthly Decay of 1-Year Call

1

A good golf partner is someone who
always plays slightly worse than you.

Each month you waited to buy this option, you would pay less. The chart shows how much less the option would cost each month. If you bought the option when it only had one month to go before it expired, you would have to pay only $1.80, and the stock would only have to go up above $71.80 before you made a profit on the option.

Most option buyers prefer to pay $1.80 for an option that only has a month of remaining life rather than $7.80 for an option that has a year of life. In the *36% Solution,* we do just the opposite.[1]

In the *36% Solution,* at the same time we *buy* options with a year or more until expiration, we *sell* someone else an option that only has a month to go until expiration. We are allowed to use our long-term option as collateral for the short term sale.

The price we pay is the spread between the two options:

Buy one-year call option for $7.80
Sell one-month call option for $1.80
Cost of spread: $6.00 ($600)

After one month, if the price of the stock remains at $70, the price of the option we bought for $7.80 will have fallen in value by about $.40, and is then worth $7.40. However, the option we sold to someone else would be worthless since the stock price is not higher than $70 and there is no time remaining for the option.

The spread that we purchased for $6.00 is now worth $7.40. We made a gain of $1.40, or about 23% on our investment in a single month (less commissions). At that point, we would sell another one-month option for $1.80 and wait for another month to expire.

If the stock remained at $70 for an entire year, and we sold a one-month option 11 more times for $1.80 a pop, we would collect $19.80 ($1980) on our original investment of $6.00 ($600), or over 300%.

The difference in the lower decay rate of the long-term option we own and the higher decay rate of the short-term option we sell is the essence of the *36% Solution.* Everything else is just details.

If you watch a game, it's fun.
If you play at it, it's recreation.
If you work at it, it's golf.

— BOB HOPE

Of course, this is a simplified example. The stock will never stay exactly flat. Sometimes it will stay almost flat, however, and we would earn over 20% in a single month in the above example.

There are three aspects to the *36% Solution*:

1) Place spreads similar to the above.
2) Buy "insurance" to protect against big stock moves. Like all insurance, it costs money and reduces our potential profits each month.
3) Make adjustments if there is a big price move (not always necessary).

We don't mind giving up a bit of potential profit to dramatically increase the odds that a reasonable profit will come our way no matter what the stock does.

We only need 3% a month to achieve our goal of 36% a year. The above example shows that there is a potential gain of over 20% in a single month if the stock doesn't do much. As long as the insurance and adjustment costs are less than 17% of portfolio value each month, we will make our goal. In most cases, these costs are considerably less than 17% of the portfolio value.

---

1. You may wonder why a one-month option costs about three times as much as the average monthly cost of a one-year option. It is a matter of demand. Option buyers are risk-takers, much like lottery ticket buyers. They like to "wager" the smallest amount possible (regardless of the odds of winning), and the one-month option is their ticket of choice. Their demand pushes up the price of the shortest-term, least-expensive options. In many respects, when we employ the *36% Solution*, we are like the house in Las Vegas, accepting wagers from the speculators, knowing that the odds are always in our favor.

Golf is played by twenty million mature American men whose wives think they are out having fun.

— JIM BISHOP

HOLE 12

Writing Covered Calls Doesn't Work

Many financial advisors and more than a dozen websites advocate writing (selling) covered calls as a sound investment strategy. Thousands of subscribers pay millions of dollars to get advice on profitable covered calls to write.

I believe they are wasting their money. Writing covered calls only limits the potential gain you might enjoy.

Let's take an example. You buy 100 shares of XYZ for $80 and write (sell) an at-the-money two-month call ($80 strike price) for $4.00. If the stock stays flat, you will earn 5% on your money for the period (plus collect a dividend if there is one). If you can do this six times a year (write a two-month call six times), you will earn 30% annually (less commissions); or so goes the promise.

(We saw in the last chapter that selling calls against a one-year option rather than stock results in a hypothetical 300% gain if the stock stays absolutely flat, or ten times the amount you could earn by writing calls against the stock.)

In this covered call-writing example, 30% is the maximum amount you can earn. No matter how high XYZ goes in price, you can never earn more than 30%. And **the bottom line truth is that you will NEVER earn that 30%**. The reason is that no stock price ever stays the same. If the stock goes up by $5 in the first 60 days, you will either lose your stock (through exercise), or more likely, you will buy back the call you wrote, paying $5, and losing $1 on the call (but making $5 on the increase in the price of the stock). So for the first 60 days, you actually made a 5% net gain ($4 net gain on a $80 stock).

Presumably, you then sell another 60-day at-the-money call (now at the $85 strike) and collect perhaps $4.25. Then the stock falls back to $80. In this time period, you gain $4.25 from selling the call but you lose $5 in stock value for a net loss of $.75.

Your gains on the calls you wrote now total $3.25 for a 120-day period (you gained $4.00 in the first 60-day period and lost $.75 in

I'm hitting the woods just great,
but I'm having a terrible time getting out of them.

— Harry Toscano

the second). The stock is now just where it started (just what you hoped would earn you 30% for the year).

At this rate (four months of activity), your annual return will be $9.75, or 12.2% on the original $80 stock. Commissions on six sales of calls over the year will considerably reduce this return — to 10% or so. Not a bad return, but certainly not 30%. And it's an awful lot of work for a 10% return.

What is even better than writing covered calls? The *36% Solution*, of course. This strategy can make over 36% a year in good years and bad. It involves buying long-term options and selling short-term options against them at several different strike prices.

At the beginning of 2003, I put $10,000 in an account to demonstrate to *Terry's Tips* (my Internet newsletter) subscribers how a strategy of buying long-term options and selling short term options against them might work. I called this the *10K Strategy*.[1] It was designed to earn 100% a year in a flat or up market. I decided to invest exclusively in the NASDAQ 100 tracking stock (QQQQ) to avoid the difficult decision of picking the right underlying stock.

By the end of the year, the account had grown in value to over $29,600, an incredible increase of over 196%.

Has anyone ever made 196% in a single year by writing covered calls? I don't think so. But every single person who followed my advice in 2003 made 196% with my *10K Strategy* (the same strategy I used, with a few tweaks, to make over 200% on Fannie Mae while the stock fell by 8.6%). See every trade I made in Fannie Mae at **www.Terrys-Tips.com** by signing up for the free newsletter.

This same strategy earned an average annualized gain of 103% for 8 actual portfolios I offered in 2005 and over 50% on 10 portfolios in 2006.

The *36% Solution* is a modification of the *10K Strategy*. Instead of going for 100% a year, it aims at a lower return with a much higher likelihood of achieving that more reasonable goal every year.

---

1. I called it the *10K Strategy* because it wasn't a sprint (like day-trading) nor was it a marathon (where you had to wait a very long time to see results).

1

Golf isn't a game, it's a choice
that one makes with one's life.

— Charles Rosin,
Northern Exposure: Aurora Borealis

Finding the Right Underlying

While the *36% Solution* can be used with the options of almost any underlying stock, there are important reasons why certain underlying stocks are far better than others.

As we have seen, the enemy of the *36% Solution* is volatility. Since a large gain is always made if the stock stays absolutely flat, the best choice would seem to be a stock that just doesn't move very much. And for sure, there are a lot of them out there. We all have probably owned them for years.

The problem with such stable stocks is that the market recognizes that they don't fluctuate much, and the option prices are dreadfully low, so low that the strategy just doesn't work.

Some stocks do fluctuate a lot, such as Apple Computer and Google, and option prices on these stocks are considerably higher. However, when earnings announcements are made (or any of the other possible events mentioned in Chapter 2), the stock often surges or drops suddenly, and wipes out potential profits overnight.

The challenge is to find an underlying stock that has relatively high option premiums but is not subject to sudden price changes. The solution is not really a stock at all, but an Exchange Traded Fund (ETF) that is composed of a large number of different stocks.

The larger the number of stocks in the ETF, the less likely a big stock price move will come about because of what happens to an individual company.

After kicking the tires of many ETFs over the years, I have concluded that one stands out above all the others. It is the Russell 2000 Index. Started in 1984, the Russell 2000 Index is a subset of the larger Russell 3000. It is one of the most widely used indexes by investors and is generally accepted as the benchmark for small-cap firms. It includes many newer, smaller firms that are not represented by the S&P 500 or other large indexes.

Golf is like a love affair.
If you don't take it seriously, it's no fun;
if you do take it seriously, it breaks your heart.

— Arthur Daley

Though the index contains smaller, more volatile companies, the Russell 2000 has handily outperformed its large-cap peers since its inception. It trades more shares than all the other Russell ETFs put together.

The options for IWM are also actively traded and quite liquid, and strikes are available at every dollar increment so we can fine-tune our risk level more precisely. There are small differences between bid and asked prices for the options, so you don't pay a huge transaction cost when buying or selling. (I call this cost the bid-asked-spread-penalty — it becomes extremely important when you are trading large numbers of individual options as we do in the *36% Solution*).

Best of all, the prices for the long-term options we buy are usually "cheap" compared to the relatively "expensive" short-term options we sell. For investors in the *36% Solution* this results in a "decay advantage" (see Appendix A for a discussion of what makes an option price "cheap" or "expensive").

While IWM is our favorite underlying ETF, we also have had good luck with the Dow Jones Industrial Average tracking stock (DIA, better known as Diamonds), the S&P 500 tracking stock (SPY), and for a little foreign diversification, the Emerging Markets ETF (EEM) which consists of larger companies in over 20 emerging countries with a concentration in BRIC (Brazil, Russia, India, and China).

We also have used the Oil Services ETF (OIH) which is a narrow-based index made up of only 18 companies in the same industry. OIH options have high premiums because volatility is high, and this ETF often behaves more like an individual (and volatile) stock rather than an ETF.

1

Money will come to you when you
are doing the right thing.

— MICHAEL PHILLIPS

Playing golf is the right thing to do.

— ATTRIBUTED TO SEVERAL THOUSAND GOLF NUTS, SO FAR.

HOLE 14

Setting Up the 36% Solution

There are two variations of the *36% Solution* — the *Diagonal Variation* which uses in-the-money LEAPS for the long positions and the *Multiple Calendar Variation* which involves buying options with fewer months of remaining life at several strike prices both above and below the stock price.

Both variations are based on the primary premise of this book — that options have different decay rates, and profits can be gained by buying slow-decaying longer-term options and selling faster-decaying short-term options. However, each variation goes about protecting against the common enemy, volatility, in a different manner.

For six months, we tested both variations as a method of achieving the modest goal of the *36% Solution* (a steady 36% gain each year regardless of which way the market goes). The *Multiple Calendar Variation* proved to be too volatile for our purposes (in one month it lost 20%, and in another, it gained over 30%).

Based on our experience, we decided to discontinue this variation as a method of carrying out the *36% Solution*. (We retained the portfolio as *Russell 2000 – 1* with a starting value of $10,000, and set up essentially the same positions in the *Russell 2000 – 3* with a starting value of $5,000). Appendix E reports how these portfolios have performed since their inception (and for a more current update, go to **www.TerrysTips.com/TrackRecord**).

The *Diagonal Variation* is carried out in two different portfolios, one using calls and the other using puts. To avoid the possibility of hopelessly confusing this discussion, we will go through setting up the *36% Solution* using calls instead of puts. (Our *36% Solution – Calls* portfolio has a longer track record although the *36% Solution – Puts* portfolio has recorded a nearly identical annualized percentage gain at the time of this writing).

The first step in setting up a *36% Solution* portfolio is to select LEAPS with at least a year or two of remaining life. When we set up

Most people are beat up by the market
instead of beating the market.

— MARK T. HEBNER

the *36% Solution – Calls* portfolio in February 2007, we selected call LEAPS that expired in January 2009, so that we had 23 months of life where we could sell short-term calls.

While there is no magical formula that can be used to decide exactly which strike prices to choose, our preference was to select some slightly in-the-money and some at-the-money strikes. This choice did not tie up a lot of unnecessary cash (as deep in-the-money LEAPS would require) yet allowed us a little slack if the stock were to fall and we wanted to sell short-term calls at lower strikes. (You can't sell short-term calls at strike prices which are lower than your LEAP strikes without incurring a maintenance requirement by your broker).

In February 2007 we opened a $10,000 account at *thinkorswim* and with IWM trading at $81, we purchased January 2009 call LEAPS at the 77, 79, and 81 strikes, and sold March 2007 calls at the 79, 81, and 83 strikes. This is the Trade Alert we sent out to subscribers:

BTO (Buy to Open) 3 Jan09 77 calls
STO (Sell to Open) 3 Mar07 79 calls
 (as a spread for a debit of $9.90)

BTO (Buy to Open) 4 Jan09 79 calls
STO (Sell to Open) 4 Mar07 81 calls
 (as a spread for a debit of $10.00)

BTO (Buy to Open) 3 Jan09 81 calls
STO (Sell to Open) 3 Mar07 83 calls
 (as a spread for a debit of $9.80)

We could have entered orders to buy the LEAPS first, and then sold the March calls afterwards, but that would have required more cash than we had. By placing spread orders, you only have to come up with the difference in the cash you need to lay out to buy the LEAPS and the proceeds you get from selling the short-term calls.

*In baseball you hit your home run over
the right-field fence, the left-field fence,
the center-field fence. Nobody cares.
In golf everything has got to
be right over second base.*

— KEN HARRELSON

Once the trades were executed, our positions looked like this:

Long positions:	Short positions:
3 Jan09 77 calls ($12.70) – $3,810	3 Mar07 79 calls ($2.90) – ($870)
4 Jan09 79 calls ($11.50) – $4,600	4 Mar07 81 calls ($1.70) – ($680)
3 Jan09 81 calls ($10.40) – $3,120	3 Mar07 83 calls ($.90) – ($270)

Total value of Portfolio: $9,710

When you first set up a portfolio, your total account value falls immediately (by about 3 to 5%) because of the bid-asked-spread-penalty, but this is usually overcome within a couple of weeks when the decay advantage has had some time to do its thing.

Note that the average time premium of the 10 LEAPS was $9.53 ($8.70 for the 77 calls, $9.50 for the 79 calls, and $10.40 for the 81 calls). Since there are 23 months of remaining life to these call LEAPS, the average monthly decay was $.41.

For the 10 March calls that we sold, the average time premium was $1.22 ($.90 for the 3 March 79 calls, $1.70 for the 4 March 81 calls, and $.90 for the 3 March 83 calls). This means that if the stock stayed at $81, the LEAPS would decay at the rate of $.41 each month while the March 2007 calls we sold to other people would decay by $1.22 for the month, so we would gain $810 ($1.22 – $.41 = $.81 x 100 x 10 contracts) for the month if the stock did not fluctuate.

The risk profile graph on page 75 shows that our actual gain in the first month if the stock stayed at $81 would be closer to $1000 than $810 because so early in their life, the LEAPS would decay at a lower rate than the average decay for all 23 months:

During 2007, IWM generally traded lower than the $81 price it enjoyed in February. In November, it was selling in the low $70's, and we were forced to sell the Jan09 81 LEAPS and replace them with Jan09 74 and 75 LEAPS so we could continue to collect at-the-money time premium each month. However, we were able to retain the Jan09 77 and 79 LEAPS throughout the year.

1

Why not go out on a limb?
Isn't that where the fruit is?

— FRANK SCULLY

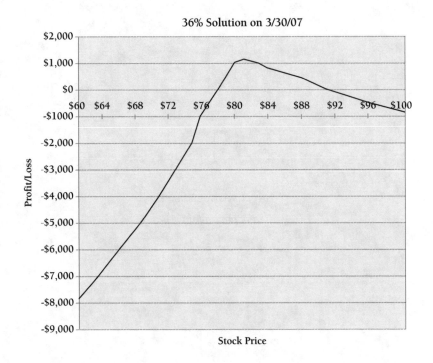

36% Solution on 3/30/07

We sold enough short-term premium during the first ten months so that we could withdraw $5400 from the portfolio and still have an account worth over $10,000. (See the complete record of all *Terry's Tips* portfolios in Appendix E.)

Forget your opponents;
always play against par.

— SAM SNEAD

HOLE 15
Making Adjustments

O nce the original positions are established in the *36% Solution,* adjustments are required every month. Most of these adjustments occur just before the current month short options are about to expire. Other adjustments sometimes become necessary when the stock price moves too much in one direction, and you will need to buy some "insurance" to protect against a further move in that same direction.

In both cases, the key to deciding which adjustments are appropriate can be found using a risk profile graph such as this one:

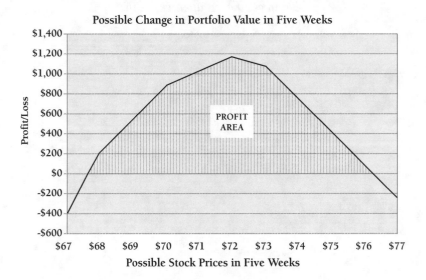

This graph is a typical depiction of the profit or loss that will accrue when the short options expire in a five-week expiration month. At the time of this graph's creation, the stock was trading at $72. The portfolio value at the time was $10,000. You can see that if the stock ends up in five weeks between $68.50 and $75.20, the $300 monthly profit goal will be achieved. If you are lucky enough to see the stock end up very near to $72, more than triple that profit amount could result.

The real test in golf and in life is not
in keeping out of the rough,
but in getting out after we are in.

— JOHN H. MOORE

The break-even range for the stock is $67.60 to $76. For the stock to move outside this range, it would mean that it moved by over 5% in that month. Over the past three years, IWM has changed by 5% or more in only six months out of 36. If no mid-month adjustments were made, this would mean that 83% of the time, a profit would result. Mid-month "insurance" adjustments might eliminate the losses in some of the 17% of the months where a loss might otherwise result.

Every time a trade is made in the actual account where we trade the *36% Solution* at *Terry's Tips*, we create a new risk profile graph similar to the above so that we can easily see how we will do as the stock price changes.

If you choose to use the *36% Solution* on your own, you should purchase the Excel software package that is used to create this graph. It was developed by a young man who lives in Argentina and only costs $37.90. As a special offer, readers of this book can order it at **http://www.kaininito.com/optioncalculator** with a $5 discount. (I have recommended him so often that he offers a discount to people I send along).

This software does everything I want and more, and most of all, is easy to use. What I like best about it is that once you enter your positions, you click an update button, the current market prices are looked up for you, and the graph updated.

You can probably guess how I use the graphing software almost every day to manage my positions. I play what-if games to see what the portfolio would look like if I changed the options that I currently owned or sold to someone else. Usually this means altering the strike prices or expiration of the short options. (Once the LEAPS are in place, they are rarely sold.)

These what-if studies are exactly what I use to decide which changes I want to make to achieve my goal of a reasonable profit each month and an extremely high likelihood of making that profit.

As a guide to which adjustments should be made, I have established the following Adjustment Trading Rules to help in managing the positions in the *36% Solution* portfolio:

*If profanity had an influence on the flight
of the ball, the game of golf would
be played far better than it is.*

— HORACE G. HUTCHINSON

1) When the average daily decay of the current month option (the asked price) is less than the average daily decay of the next-month same-strike option (the bid price), roll over to the next month by buying back the current month option and selling the next-month same-strike option. (Sometimes different strikes are sold for the next month, but this average daily decay calculation is based on the same strike options for the two months.)

   For example, if there are 10 days remaining until the September expiration (and 38 days until the October expiration) and you are short a September 72 option (bid $.05 — asked $.10), you would calculate the average daily decay by dividing $10 ($.10 x 100) by the number of remaining days (10) to get $1.00. (The *asked* price is used because you would have to buy back that option if you were to roll over to the next month.)

   If the October 72 option is bid $.50 — asked $.60, the average daily decay would be $50/38 days, or $1.31. It would be time to roll over to the October series. (For the October option, you would use the *bid* price because you would sell it if you were rolling over from September to October.)

2) On expiration Friday, buy back any in-the-money options and replace them with next-month options. Choose strike prices that will leave you with short options at strike prices in the same ratio as the original positions (i.e., a majority at the money, and slightly fewer in the money and out of the money).

3) On expiration Friday, if the stock price is within $.50 of a strike price, and your short option is out of the money, if it is a call, buy it back and sell the next month same-strike call. If your short option is a put, let the current out-of-the-money option expire worthless and wait until Monday to sell the next-month same-strike put. Stock prices tend to trade lower on the Monday following an expiration, and better *put* prices can often be obtained on Monday while better *call* prices are usually available on Friday.

*Never keep more than 20 separate thoughts
in your mind during your swing.*

— Anon.

4) When the strike price of a LEAP becomes 8% higher or lower than the stock price, sell that LEAP and replace it with one at a strike price closer to the stock price, using the risk profile graphing software to help determine the best strike for your current configuration of options. (The 8% number changes to 10% for more volatile underlying stocks, i.e., those with implied volatilities of 30% or more.)

5) LEAP Adjustments: It is difficult to set down in advance a complete program for selling the original LEAPS and replacing them with different strike prices and LEAPS with longer life spans. If the market moves dramatically higher, the existing call LEAPS might be so far in the money that they consume too much cash, and will need to be replaced by higher-strike (and probably longer out) LEAPS. On the other hand, if puts are employed, a rising market means that short-term puts at the lowest strike of the LEAPS may not have sufficient time premium, and will need to be replaced by higher-strike spreads.

Generally, LEAPS are sold no sooner than four months before they expire, and replaced with longer-term LEAPS. Of course, when they only have four months of remaining life, they are not called LEAPS any longer.

"Insurance" purchases: In addition to these adjustments, a small amount of cash (perhaps 5% of portfolio value) should be retained for possible "insurance" purchases. An example of such a purchase would be if the stock went up strongly and has moved dangerously close to the break-even point on the risk profile graph. An insurance purchase would be to buy the next-month-out option and sell the current month option at a strike at least $2 higher than the break-even stock price on the risk profile graph.

It doesn't matter whether you buy puts or calls at this higher strike, although the put spreads will cost you less, and you can buy more

⛳ 1

*The golf swing is like a suitcase
into which we are trying to pack
one too many things.*

— JOHN UPDIKE

spreads (and gain more protection) for the same amount of cash if you buy puts rather than calls.

These particular spreads are purchased because they are the least expensive way you can add short positions at higher strikes. At expiration, the greatest gain is with those short options you have exactly at a strike price. They will expire worthless (or nearly so), and the next-month option at that same strike price will have more time premium than any other option in that monthly series.

If you do not have spare cash with which to buy this kind of "insurance," you can usually generate cash by "rolling over" some of the options according to the above Trading Rules. When the stock moves strongly higher, your short options at the lowest strike prices will likely trigger a roll-over because of the average daily decay comparison.

These adjustments may seem confusing at this point. Once you have managed the *36% Solution* for a few months, they will seem simple and routine.

Note: It is not always possible to follow the above rules precisely. Rather, they should be used as a guide for putting on and taking off positions. Short-term technical measures might cause you to deviate from these Trading Rules, or external downside events such as 9/11 would call for suspension of the 8% adjustment tactic (Rule 4) since the market almost always recovers fairly quickly from such events.

Lack of money is the root of all evil.

— GEORGE BERNARD SHAW

Trading Options in Your IRA

S ince I believe that the *36% Solution* involves less risk than buying stock or mutual funds, I believe that trading stock options is a totally appropriate investment for your IRA.

In addition to the lower risk, there is one major financial reason to trade the *36% Solution* in your IRA rather than a regular investment account — most of the profits are taxed as short-term capital gains.

Occasionally, you can enjoy the benefits of long-term capital gains taxation while using this strategy. When you first purchase LEAPS, they have two or more years until they expire. If the stock moves strongly in one direction (up for call LEAPS, or down for put LEAPS), and you hold on to these LEAPS for at least one year, when you sell them, you will enjoy long-term capital gains treatment.

However, most of the profits come from the short-term options that you sell. These options go down in value from decay, and you usually buy them back for a lower price than you sold them for, or they expire worthless, and the entire proceeds of your sale is taxable as a short-term capital gain. From a tax standpoint, it might as well be ordinary income.

Since most people think that stock options are risky investments, they can't fathom trading them in their IRAs. If you have read my arguments in this little book, maybe you can see that managing options with a strategy such as the *36% Solution* might be *less* risky than owning stock. After all, if the stock falls a little, you can still make money with this strategy while a falling stock will always result in a loss with a traditional stock purchase.

Unfortunately, many brokerage firms do not allow their customers to trade options in their IRA accounts. I believe they have this policy because they do not understand the options business, or if they do, they don't trust their customers to trade options responsibly. Even if such option trading is less risky than owning stocks or mutual funds, most brokers prohibit such activity in IRA accounts.

*Some people throw their clubs backwards,
and that's wrong. You should always throw a club
ahead of you so that you don't have to walk
any extra distance to get it.*

— TOMMY BOLT

HOLE 17

Find the Right Discount Broker

I f you want to trade options, you need to find an Internet-based discount broker who is options-friendly, has low commission rates, and allows option trading in your IRA. In addition, unless you want to deal with the hassle of placing all the orders yourself, the broker should have an Auto-Trade* system in place.

There are fewer than a dozen firms that meet the above requirements. I have checked them all out thoroughly. I worked with several of these firms for many years, and one of them eventually proved superior to the others on just about every possible dimension.

This Chicago brokerage firm goes by the unlikely name *thinkorswim*. You can find them at **http://www.thinkorswim.com.**

For a year and a half, (through *Terry's Tips*) I sent Trade Alerts (recommendations) to several brokers who had Auto-Trade programs. Then I discovered that *thinkorswim* consistently got better prices than any of the other brokers. Sometimes they saved my subscribers hundreds of dollars on a single trade.

I think there is a reason for their superior executions. Most online brokers place orders electronically through an automated ordering system. Unlike most on-line discount brokers, *thinkorswim* has an actual trade desk. Many of their brokers have over 20 years experience trading on the floor of the CBOE. For larger orders, such as the collective orders placed through Auto-Trade, a broker at *thinkorswim* telephones the orders directly to a specialist on the floor of an exchange (someone he probably knows personally), and often negotiates better prices than can be achieved on an electronic platform.

---

* Auto-Trade is a mechanism where you authorize your broker to place trades in your account based on the recommendations of a newsletter or advisor who you select. Trades executed through Auto-Trade do not cost anything more than their normal commission rates, and executions are often made at lower prices than an individual could get with a trade on his own.

*It is almost impossible to remember
how tragic a place this world is
when one is playing golf.*

— ROBERT LYND

At *thinkorswim* you will find the best analytic software around and real-time stock and option quotes, all free. I also like their order entry screen. You don't have to remember the option symbols to place an order, for example. That is a big benefit for me — I hate those gibberish symbols. Even more important, you don't have to remember whether you are making an opening or closing trade — they keep track of it for you. Most online brokers make you figure it out for yourself.

New option traders will find that they really hold your hand while explaining how to get started at *thinkorswim*, They offer great personal service (and no extra charges for telephone orders). A simple phone call will get you set up for one of their Auto-Trade portfolios without your having to enter any orders. I don't know of another broker who offers this service.

You are offered a choice of commission plans at *thinkorswim* — their own, which has lower rates for very small orders, or you can select the same commission schedule offered by several other discount brokers.

There are a few other firms who have lower commission rates, but they have serious shortcomings as well. Most of them do not have Auto-Trade programs and more importantly, they do not have a good system for handling early exercise of short options that sometimes occurs. I have a collection of horror stories sent to me by my newsletter subscribers concerning some of these brokers.

Several brokers have asked me to participate in their Auto-Trade program by sending them my Trade Alerts as they are issued. (Of course, their clients would be *Terry's Tips* Premium Service Insiders.) While I understand that my business might expand considerably if I took them up on their offers, I have decided, at least at this point, to decline their invitations.

My reasons are two-fold — first, I am reluctant to expand my staff (we are a very small and skilled team that has been together for over four years, with every member working from his or her own home here in Vermont). Second, I believe that *thinkorswim* offers the absolute best package of trading platforms, free analytic software, commission rates, and executions, and I suspect that participating in

Change is inevitable,
except from a vending machine.

other brokers' Auto-Trade programs would be considered to be a tacit endorsement of that brokerage.

I will continue to monitor other firms to see if their service improves to match that of *thinkorswim*, and let my newsletter subscribers know if another good alternative comes along. So far, it hasn't.

1

What a wonderful day we've had.
You have learned something,
and I have learned something.
Too bad we didn't learn it sooner.
We could have played golf instead. ...

— Balki Bartokomous,
(paraphrased) *Perfect Strangers*

Summary of the 36% Solution

The *36% Solution* is an options strategy that is based on the simple idea that long-term options (LEAPS) have considerably lower decay values than short-term options. The strategy consists of owning LEAPS and using them as collateral to sell short-term options to others. Over time, as long as the underlying stock or ETF does not fluctuate too much, a gain is made every month because of the difference in decay rates. The strategy may involve either puts or calls, and has clearly-defined Adjustment Trading Rules to contend with volatility when it occurs.

In 2007, we established two separate *36% Solution* portfolios, one employing puts and one employing calls. In the middle of December, both portfolios had increased in value at the exact same annualized rate (and that rate was an astounding 59%). Cash was withdrawn each month (whenever a 3% gain had been made) so that the portfolio value remained close to $10,000 in value.*

Lower Risk Profile. The *36% Solution* involves less risk than most of the portfolios carried out at *Terry's Tips*. Since options are leveraged investments, risks are inherently greater than traditional investments. Otherwise, the lofty returns sought by *Terry's Tips* subscribers would not be possible. However, the *36% Solution* is designed to modify risk in several ways:

• Buying true LEAPS (usually two years or more) for the long side so that there is plenty of time to recover from short-term adverse movements in the stock price.

---

* The portfolios referred to are ones maintained for subscribers to *Terry's Tips*. They are actual portfolios where positions are monitored and reported each week to subscribers. If the portfolios have a losing month, no money is removed from them. On the other hand, if a portfolio gains more than $300 in one expiration month, additional withdrawls in increments of $300 are made. Of course, subscribers may choose a multiple of $10,000 amounts for their own portfolios, and also choose not to remove money from their portfolio if they wish.

The real teacher is you.
You're the one who must decide,
of all that comes your way,
what is true and what is not.

— JOHN-ROGER AND PETER MCWILLIAMS,
LIFE 101

- Selling short-term options at several different strikes so that the risk is spread over a range of possible stock prices.
- Following a pre-determined set of Adjustment Trading Rules when volatility does take place.

Selection of the Underlying. The *36% Solution* uses the Russell 2000 (Small Cap) ETF as the underlying stock. Options on IWM are ideal for our purposes, as they are quite liquid and have small bid-asked spreads so we can get good executions. Also, strikes are available at every dollar increment which allows for precise management of risk.

The Composite Market Timing Model. The Composite Market Timing Model is a proprietary model developed by *Terry's Tips*. It is based on several market-timing resources (mostly paid Internet publications) that employ different technical or behavioral variables to determine whether the market is trending up or down. We have found that our composite model is more accurate than any other single model that is included as part of our composite model.

Since IWM is a composite of 2000 small-cap companies, general market trend is the over-riding factor that determines whether the stock will be going up or down. We need to pay strict attention to the direction indicated by our Composite Market Timing Model as we adjust our risk profile over time.

Puts vs. Calls in the *36% Solution*. Late in August 2006 I waited until IWM was trading at exactly $70 so that I could compare the prices of the at-the-money September puts and calls. At that time, the Sep06 70 calls were bid at $1.45 while the Sep06 70 puts were bid at $1.30, a $.15 difference.

At that same time, the Jan09 70 LEAPS were asking $11.40 for the calls and only $7.70 for the puts. If someone bought the Jan09 70–Sep06 call spread, the natural price (i.e. buying at the asked price and selling at the bid price) would be $9.95, and the $1.45 received would be a 14.6% return on investment (ROI) in three weeks (not counting the miniscule decay of the LEAPS) if the stock stayed abso-

Oxymoron: An easy par-3.

lutely flat. On the other hand, the same spread in puts would cost only $6.40, and the $1.30 earned from selling the put would be a 20.3% return if the stock stayed flat. The put spread is clearly superior from the ROI standpoint.

However, when put spreads are used exclusively, a problem is encountered if the stock falls and the highest-strike put spreads become deep in the money. The bid-asked spread becomes quite large for these deep in-the-money spreads, and it is quite difficult to roll over to subsequent months and collect significant new premium.

To avoid the potential problem of short puts becoming too deep in the money, we tend to sell more out-of-the-money puts (i.e., at strikes below the strike price) in the put portfolios. If the stock goes up, the lower-strike short puts can be rolled up to higher strikes without additional cash being required.

If IWM moves higher most of the time, which history suggests it will, the put spreads will become out of the money at some point, and the LEAPS will have to be rolled up to higher strikes. We want to avoid trading the LEAPS if we can. The bid-asked spread is higher for LEAPS than it is for shorter-term options, so the bid-asked-spread-penalty will be greater when rolling from one LEAP to another. The disadvantage of rolling up put LEAPS to higher strikes sometimes offsets the advantage we enjoyed when they were originally purchased at a lower cost than call LEAPS would have cost.

A more detailed discussion of using *puts* rather than *calls* in calendar-type spreads is presented in Appendix B.

Making Adjustments. The biggest concern for the *36% Solution* portfolio is the one or two months each year when the stock (IWM) moves by over $4 or so. Except for unusual events such as 9/11, when large stock price changes take place, they usually take place over a week or so rather than dropping (or rising) in a single day. There should be time to make adjustments to lessen or eliminate the losses in those rare months.

We should not expect to see whipsaw-like moves in IWM (such as we have often seen in many individual stocks as good and bad news

They call it golf because all of the other
four-letter words were taken.

— RAYMOND FLOYD

sometimes buffets the stock wildly in both directions). Such rapid changes in direction are less likely, of course, when 2000 different companies are involved rather than a single company.

Adjustment Trading Rules for the *36% Solution:*

1) When the *average daily decay* of the current-month option that you have sold becomes less than the *average daily decay* of the next-month-out option at the same strike price, buy back the current-month option and sell the next-month-out option.

   The average daily decay comparison is made by dividing the asked price of the current-month option by the number of remaining days to expiration, and comparing this number to the bid price of the next-month-out option divided by the number of remaining days to expiration for that option.

   You can perform this calculation every day yourself, or let *Terry's Tips* do it for you. A Trade Alert is issued whenever the average daily decay comparison triggers an adjustment requirement.

2) When the strike price of a calendar spread becomes more than 8% higher or lower than the stock price, sell that spread and replace it with a spread which is nearer to the stock price.

3) Use the Excel Options Calculator software to determine how many short-term options should be sold at each of the possible strike prices (create a profit range that covers a stock move in either direction).

This same software is critical in setting up the positions at all times if you are following the *36% Solution* on your own rather than subscribing to *Terry's Tips* and having your broker execute trades for you through Auto-Trade.

1

He who hesitates is poor.

— MEL BROOKS, THE PRODUCERS

HOLE 19

How to Get Started

There are three different ways for you to put this strategy to work:

1) Do it on your own.
2) Subscribe to the *Terry's Tips* regular service.
3) Subscribe to the *Terry's Tips* special *36% Solution* premium service.

1) Do it on your own. If you want to carry out the *36% Solution* on your own, without ongoing guidance from *Terry's Tips*, you know what you need to do to get set up with your broker. I hope I have given you sufficient instructions on how to manage the strategy.

2) Subscribe to the *Terry's Tips* regular service. If you would like to carry out the *36% Solution* with some ongoing guidance from *Terry's Tips*, our regular subscription service involves an initial purchase of our White Paper ($79.95). This report offers a detailed description of several strategies, including the *10K Strategy* which the *36% Solution* is a modification of.

The White Paper also includes a list of 20 "Lazy Way" companies where a 100% gain is mathematically guaranteed in two years if the stock stays flat, goes up by any amount, or falls less than 5% or 10%. Most of these stocks can fall by 25% or more over the two years and a profit is also realized. It is called the "Lazy Way" strategy because only two trades are made at the beginning of the period, and then you just sit and wait it out for an average of two years. (The "Lazy Way" strategy cannot be conducted in an IRA, but all the other *Terry's Tips*' actual portfolios can be mirrored in an IRA.)

Along with the White Paper, you will receive an ongoing Options Tutorial Program with a new lesson delivered each day for 14 days. In addition, you will receive two free months of Insider access. This includes our weekly reports which describe the current positions and

*Golf is so popular simply because it is
the best game in the world at which to be bad.*

— A.A. MILNE

risk profile graphs of twelve or so actual option portfolios (including the *36% Solution* portfolios).

After these two free months, you may wish to continue with our regular subscription program at the rate of $19.95 per month.

The regular service includes Trade Alerts which are sent out at the end of the trading day for all the portfolios. These Trade Alerts include the specific trades which need to be made and the prices that should be paid.

Since these alerts are sent out at the end of the day, the prices may or may not be available in the market on the next day. However, many *Terry's Tips* subscribers have successfully mirrored our portfolios with the regular subscription service.

To get set up with the regular *Terry's Tips* service, go to **www.TerrysTips.com** and click on Sign up For Paid Services.

3) Subscribe to the *Terry's Tips* special *36% Solution* premium service. This alternative is designed for people who wish to have the *36% Solution* strategy managed in their own account for them through a broker's Auto-Trade program, or who need real-time notification of trades being made in *Terry's Tips* portfolios.

This is a simpler alternative. It does not involve buying the White Paper and learning all about trading options. Once you are set up, everything is done for you automatically, and you can head back to the golf course.

The special *36% Solution* premium service includes real-time Trade Alerts sent to you and your broker. This allows you to make trades at the actual prices that are available during the day when the alert is issued rather than waiting until the next day and hoping that those prices are still available.

This service costs $39.99 for the first month (which includes the set-up fee) and $49.98 for subsequent months. This monthly fee is the same regardless of whether you have invested $10,000 or $1,000,000 or more. It is charged directly to your credit card and is not taken out of your broker account. (Of course, *Terry's Tips* has no access to or knowledge about your account. You are free to place other trades in

Never give up.
If we give up in this game,
we give up in life.

— TOM WATSON

this same account if you wish, as long as you leave as much cash that exists in the actual *Terry's Tips 36% Solution* portfolio account that you will see updated each week).

If you want to proceed with this alternative, your first task is to open an account (IRA or regular) at **www.thinkorswim.com.**

If you want to withdraw cash from your account as we plan to do in the actual *36% Solution* account at *Terry's Tips*, you will have to initiate this withdrawal on your own. *thinkorswim* makes it easy to do online.

To get set up for the special *36% Solution* premium service at *Terry's Tips*, go to **www.TerrysTips.com/order/php**. You do not have to do this until you have set up your brokerage account, but it is a quick way to see exactly how the actual *36% Solution* account is doing, as well as the other *Terry's Tips* portfolio accounts.

This ends my explanation of the *36% Solution*. The rest of the book is for those who want to delve deeper into the details of the option world. It is not easy to explain any strategy involving options. They are derivative instruments which are complex and often confusing, and that is why very few people ever get involved with them.

In spite of the inherent complexity of options, I hope I have presented a relatively understandable explanation of why I believe this strategy has a high likelihood of achieving extraordinary investment gains year after year.

I invite you to participate in this adventure with me, and I wish both of us the best of luck on our journey together.

*Golf is a game in which you yell "fore,"
shoot six, and write down five.*

— PAUL HARVEY

Appendix A
THE GREEKS AND IMPLIED VOLATILITY

The "Greeks" are measures designed to better understand how option prices change when the underlying stock changes in value and/or time passes by (and options decline in value).

My goal is to keep this discussion of Greek measures as simple as possible. It is not easy. I have tried many times to explain these terms to people in person. I have seen their eyes glaze over before I get past *Alpha.*

I'm sure you heard about the fellow who bragged that he could speak every language except Greek, and when asked to say something in a particular foreign language, answered "It's all Greek to me." Let's hope that isn't your answer next time you are asked about a Greek stock option measure.

I'll confine this discussion to three measures of market risk exposure — *delta, gamma,* and *theta.* Mathematicians gave these measures the names of Greek letters, or names that sound like they're Greek letters (*vega,* another measure which we will not discuss here, is not in the Greek alphabet, but sounds like it should be). *Delta, gamma,* and *theta* are the three most important Greeks in the world of stock options, and each tells us something important about an option.

If you own 100 shares of a company's stock, your market risk is easy to understand. If the stock rises (or falls) by $1.00, you gain (or lose) $100. It's not so simple with stock options. The most common way to measure market risk for an option is the Greek called *delta.*

Delta is the amount the option will change in value if the stock goes up by $1.00. If an option carries a *delta* of 70, and the stock goes up by $1.00, the price of the option will rise by $.70 ($70 since each option is worth 100 shares).

Owning an option which has a *delta* of 70 means that you own the equivalent of 70 shares of the company's stock.

All options do not have the same *delta* value. Deep in-the-money options have very high *delta* values (perhaps in the 90s), while way

1

If there is any larceny in a man,
golf will bring it out.

— Paul Gallico

out-of-the-money options have very low *delta* values (could be under 10).

To make matters more confusing, *delta* values change over the life of the option, even if the price of the stock remains unchanged. An in-the-money option, which might have a *delta* value of 60 with a month to go until expiration, will have a *delta* value of essentially 100 on expiration Friday.

You can calculate the net *delta* value of your composite option positions by multiplying the *delta* value of your long options by the number of those options and subtracting the *delta* value of your short options multiplied by the number of those options. The resulting figure, net *delta* value, tells you how much the value of your current option portfolio will change if the underlying stock goes up by $1.00. It is perhaps the best measure of market risk at any given moment.

Most professional market makers who hold a variety of options in their account, some long, some short, some puts and some calls, calculate their net *delta* value continually throughout the day so that they don't expose themselves to more risk than their comfort level allows. Ideally, they like to be net *delta* neutral, which means that with their current configuration of option holdings, they do not care whether the market goes up or down.

Gamma is a measure of how much *delta* changes with a dollar change in the price of the stock. This is a more complex measure, and really shouldn't be of too much concern to you as long as you stick with the calendar spreads like those used in the *36% Solution*.

Just as with *deltas*, all *gammas* are different for different options. While you may establish a net *delta* neutral position (i.e., you don't care if the stock goes up or down), the *gamma* will most always move you away from *delta* neutrality as soon as the underlying stock changes in value.

If there is a lot of time left in an option (such as a LEAP), the *gamma* tends to be quite stable (i.e., low). This holds true for both in-the-money and out-of-the-money options. Short-term options, on

1

Man blames fate for other accidents
but feels personally responsible for
a hole in one.

— MARTHA BECKMAN

the other hand, have widely fluctuating gammas, especially when the strike price of the option is very close to the stock price.

A perfectly neutral option strategy would have a zero net *delta* position *and* a zero net *gamma* position. As long as you deal with calendar spreads, you will never enjoy this luxury. You will always see your net *delta* position fall as the stock price rises, and watch your net delta position rise as the stock price falls. *Gamma* measures tend to do the same, which serves to accelerate the change in the net *delta* position of a calendar spread portfolio.

Occasionally checking out the net *gamma* position lets you know how big the change in your net *delta* position will be if the stock moves up or down in price. It helps you know how your exposure to market risk will change as the stock price changes.

Theta is my favorite Greek, because it tells me how much money I will make today if the price of the stock stays flat. *Theta* is the amount of daily decay. It is expressed as a negative number if you own an option (that is how much your option will decay in value in one day).

On the other hand, if you are short an option, *theta* is a positive number which shows how much you will earn while the option you sold to someone else goes down in value in one day. (The *36% Solution* essentially always has a *positive net theta position*, meaning that time is on your side. It tells you exactly how many dollars you will make today if the stock stays flat. For me, knowing this number has some negative implications, however. If I'm at a restaurant on a night when the market didn't change much, I might remember the *theta* value that day — it was sort of "free" money I really didn't make any effort to earn. Oftentimes, I order a too expensive bottle of wine because of that silly *theta* number).

The ultimate goal of the *36% Solution* is to maximize the net *theta* position in your account without letting the net *delta* value get so high or low that you will lose a lot of money if the stock moves against you.

This short discussion of the Greeks should be all you need to impress your friends next time you talk about the stock market. All

1

Nothing increases your golf score like witnesses.

— ANON.

you need to do is to get around to the topic of stock options, and drop a few Greek names on them (ask them if they know what their net delta position was yesterday, or did their theta increase much last week, and watch their eyes glaze over).

I have found that the Greeks are very effective conversation stoppers. Feel free to use them whenever the need arises.

Implied Volatility

Stock option prices are determined by a variety of factors. The most important are the stock price in relation to the strike price, the length of time until expiration, the interest rate (because an option saves you much of the investment required to purchase the stock), and the dividend of the stock. All of these factors are precisely measurable at any given point in time.

Yet if two different stocks have identical numbers for all of the above variables, their option prices may differ by a considerable amount. The reason is Implied Volatility (IV) of the option.

IV is the market's estimate of how much the price of the underlying stock will fluctuate in a year. It is expressed as a percentage. If an option has an IV of 30, this means the market expects the stock to fluctuate by 30% in either direction over the course of a year. IV is usually closely related to the historic volatility of the stock unless unusual events are expected for the company. (Historic volatility for all stocks which have options can be found at the **www.cboe.com** or on the trading screen at *thinkorswim*.)

IV is the best measure of whether option prices are "high" or "low." The higher the IV, the higher the option prices. This is true for both puts and calls.

An interesting feature of option prices is that IVs are sometimes different for different option months. IV for the current month's options tends to increase shortly before important company events such as the announcement of earnings or a rumored impending acquisition. (IVs for longer-term options do not fluctuate as much when important events are imminent.)

I'm not saying my golf game went bad,
but if I grew tomatoes, they'd come up sliced.

— ATTRIBUTED TO BOTH
MILLER BARBER AND LEE TREVINO

The *36% Solution* does best if you can buy options with relatively low IVs and sell options with relatively high IVs. If you can find a spread where your long option has a lower IV than your short option, it clearly gives you a big edge.

I think there is a logical explanation for why the IVs for next-month options are often lower than any other option months — people are writing calls against their stock. Call-writers like rapid decay, and the next-month options provide the highest decay rates. If a large number of people are writing calls (or buying calendar spreads as the *36% Solution* does), the prices of the short-term call options would become relatively depressed. In the case of calendar spreads, longer-term options are being purchased, pushing those option prices up (as well as their IVs).

For many companies, IVs do not escalate prior to an earnings announcement because earnings are relatively predictable. But for companies such as Apple Computer (where quarterly earnings often fluctuate considerably) and Google (where company management doesn't tell analysts much about expected earnings), current-month option IV often skyrockets shortly before earnings announcements.

IV is an important factor in the success of the *36% Solution*. Profits can be made with the strategy even if IV is not on your side, but you gain a huge advantage when you have it. When the IV for the short-term options (which the *36% Solution* is short) is greater than the IV of the longer-term options (which the *36% Solution* is long), we call this an IV Advantage. It allows you to buy relatively cheap options and sell relatively expensive options. While an IV Advantage is often difficult to find, it is worth looking for whenever you are considering a new company to trade using the *36% Solution*.

They say golf is like life, but don't believe them.
Golf is more complicated than that.

— GARDNER DICKINSON

Appendix B
WHY PUTS ARE BETTER THAN CALLS FOR CALENDAR SPREADS

When you think of calls, you think about hoping the stock will go up. When you think of puts, you think about hoping the stock will go down. Those thoughts are appropriate when you are buying options. But they most certainly are wrong when you are buying calendar spreads.

When buying calendar spreads (also called time spreads), the *strike price* tells you which way you want the stock to go, not the choice of puts or calls. You always want the stock to move toward the strike price of your calendar spreads. That is where the maximum gain will take place, regardless of whether you own *puts* or *calls*.

There are two reasons why puts are a better choice than calls for calendar spreads:

1) The premium decay difference (the difference between the decay of the long-term options you own and the short-term options you have sold) is essentially the same for put and call spreads.
2) The put spreads cost less (usually in the neighborhood of 25% less) than the call spreads at the same strike price.

In the graphs on page 121, I have compared the risk profile of a typical calendar spread portfolio using calls and the same calendar spreads using puts. These spreads were set up for Sears Holdings (SHLD) at the 110, 120, and 130 strikes (at a time when SHLD was trading about $119). The long positions had seven months until expiration and the short positions had two months until expiration. Note the essentially identical curves. It truly does not matter whether you are trading in puts or calls from a payoff basis at each possible stock price.

Since puts and calls are opposites, our intuition would tell us that the options could not possibly achieve nearly identical returns if you used either puts or calls. But calendar spreads are entirely different from a strategy of only buying the options.

I've spent most of my life golfing...
the rest I've just wasted.

— AUTHOR UNKNOWN

醐醐醐

Risk Profile Graphs — Two Months Out

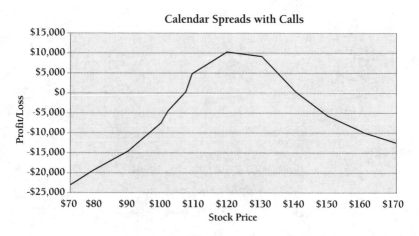

Calendar Spreads with Calls

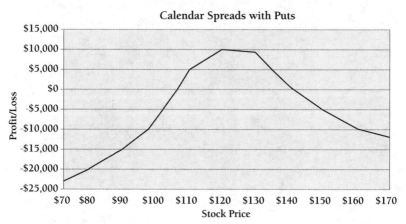

Calendar Spreads with Puts

However, there is a major advantage to picking puts over calls. The 30 spreads in the above SHLD example would have cost $24,500 to buy with calls, and only $18,650 with puts. Both charts show a maximum profit of about $10,000 if the stock closes exactly at $120 on expiration, yet the put spreads cost 24% less to place, so the ROI for the puts would be 54% (at the maximum possible gain) compared to 41% if calls were used instead.

醐醐醐

1

Duffers who consistently shank their balls
are urged to buy and study
Shanks — No Thanks *by R.K. Hoffman,*
or in extreme cases,
M.S. Howard's excellent Tennis for Beginners.

— HENRY BEARD, GOLFING, 1985

When you buy calendar spreads, you should purchase them at the strike price where you think the stock is headed. If you are bullish about the stock, you buy calendar spreads at strike prices that are higher than the stock price. If you are bearish on a stock, you buy calendar spreads at strike prices that are lower than the stock price. In the *36% Solution*, we buy calendar spreads that are above, below, and at the stock price to give us protection in both directions — we are not tied to the stock moving in only one direction.

Modification of the "puts are best" policy: For strike prices that are quite a bit higher than the stock price, it is better to buy call calendar spreads rather than put calendar spreads in spite of their higher cost. The reason is that the short-term puts are well in the money, and are quite costly. This high price means that they are not traded very actively. With inactively-traded options, a large bid-asked spread usually results. This means that you incur a large bid-asked-spread-penalty when rolling over soon-to-expire put options to the next month out. Sometimes, it is even difficult to roll over these options at a credit. For this reason, many *Terry's Tips* portfolios involve owning call spreads at the highest strike prices and put spreads at other strike prices.

It is more satisfying to be a bad player at golf.
The worse you play, the better you
remember the occasional good shot.

— Nubar Gulbenkian

Appendix C
A NOTE ON EARLY EXERCISE
OF SHORT OPTIONS

Should you worry about having your short options exercised?

The short answer is "no." The long answer is also "no."

First-time option traders are often frightened by the specter of someone taking away their stock by exercising an in-the-money call. Many feel that they must maintain a large cash reserve to protect against such an event.

Many of these fears are based on their experience of owning stock and writing calls against the stock — early exercise results in their losing the stock (and incurring a taxable event if their original cost was lower).

In the option market, these fears are unfounded.

The holder of the option is almost always better off selling an option rather than exercising it. For example, if someone owns a soon-to-expire 80 call, and the price of the stock is $81, he could exercise his option and get the stock, making a $1 profit (less what he originally paid for the option, of course). Or he could sell the option for at least $1.50 or more, depending upon how much time there is until expiration. Right up to the last hour, there will be a time premium in that option that he would lose if he exercised rather than sold the option.

Only if you fall asleep or are lost without a phone in Antarctica will you have your stock taken from you when you don't want to.

At least this is true if you are trading options in liquid, (i.e., active) markets. In some inactive option markets, there are inefficiencies. The option market for an inactive stock may be entirely controlled by a single market-maker who is greedy, and not willing to pay a time premium close to expiration. In these markets, it may be necessary for an option holder to exercise to get the price he deserves.

*I know I am getting better at golf
because I'm hitting fewer spectators.*

— GERALD FORD

What happens if you are exercised?

In the event that an exercise does take place, you should celebrate! You actually come out better than if you had to buy back the short option. Exercise eliminates the time premium you would have to pay. Your actual net cost is the intrinsic value of the option (the difference between the stock price and the strike price).

So what if you are employing the *36% Solution*, and you own a call LEAP rather than stock? In this case, your broker will sell (short) enough shares to satisfy the option-owner's desire to get the stock at the strike price. The very next day, you will have short stock in your account as well as the cash the option-exerciser paid to get those shares. You simply buy back the short stock, using the money that was paid to you when you sold it short.

Let's use an example. You have sold 10 July 80 call options short, and the stock is selling at $81 just before expiration. If you bought back these options, they would be selling at just above $1 — let's say $1.25 since there is still time premium in options up until expiration. It would cost you $1250 plus commissions to buy back the options.

If you get exercised, you sell the 1000 shares short for $80 each, or $80,000 less the commission ($15 or less at most discount brokers). You then buy back the 1000 shares in the market for $81, paying $81,000 plus commission. Your net cost was $1000 plus commissions rather than the $1250 plus commissions you would have paid if you had purchased back the options instead.

This works in an IRA as well, even though you are not technically allowed to short stock in an IRA. Your broker will insist that you buy back the short stock on the very next day, however.

Will I lose my LEAPS?

If you are lost in an African jungle on expiration Friday, and your short option is exercised because you do not buy back an in-the-money expiring call option, your broker will still not look to your LEAPS for payment. Instead, the proper number of shares of stock will be

*Golf is a game in which the slowest people
in the world are those in front of you,
and the fastest are those behind you.*

sold short in your account, and you will be asked to cover them (buy them back) on Monday.

If you are still lost in the jungle, your broker will buy the short shares back for you on the next trading day before ever considering a sale of your LEAPS (unless you have no other free cash in your account). **In short, your LEAPS are safe unless there are no cash or more liquid assets available for the broker to sell!** (This is exactly the same position you would be in if exercise had not taken place). Now that I have said this, I must qualify my statement by saying that *thinkorswim* would handle early exercise in this manner. I have heard horror stories from other brokerage firms where they indiscriminately liquidated other positions to cover an early exercise rather than buying back the stock with the cash sitting there. Your broker needs to be options-friendly and savvy.

One caveat. If you are short shares of stock, even for one day, and that day is the ex-dividend day (i.e., the day when owners of the stock are entitled to the dividend), you will be assessed the amount of the dividend. The only time this is likely to be any sort of problem is with the Dow Jones Industrial Average tracking stock (DIA), which pays a monthly dividend, and the ex-dividend date is on expiration Friday. The amount of the dividend is small, so it doesn't hurt much, but needs to be recognized. If you are short an in-the-money call on DIA during expiration week, it would probably be best to buy it back before Thursday.

For most stocks, a quarterly dividend is more common, and the ex-dividend date rarely coincides with the expiration date. Furthermore, on the day following an ex-dividend date, the stock usually falls by the amount of the dividend, so when you go to buy shares to cover your short stock, the price will be lower than it would have been before the dividend charge. **Once again, the net effect is about the same — whether you buy back the option or are exercised against.**

I play in the low 80s.
If it's any hotter than that,
I won't play.

— JOE E. LEWIS

Appendix D
MORE ABOUT THE RUSSELL 2000

The Russell 2000 Index (IWM). Started in 1984, the Russell 2000 Index is a subset of the larger Russell 3000. It is one of the most widely used indexes by investors and is generally accepted as the benchmark for small-cap firms. It includes many newer, smaller firms that are not represented by the S&P 500 or other large indexes.

The Russell 2000 Index contains the smallest 2000 stocks (based on market cap) held by the Russell 3000. Though it contains twice as many stocks as the large-cap Russell 1000, because of their small average size, its component stocks account for just 7% of the value of all U.S. equities. The index is computed based on a market cap weighting, meaning that the largest stocks have the greatest influence on the index's returns. The Russell 2000 Index is more evenly weighted than most, as the top 10 holdings represent less than 2% of the index's overall value. The average firm carries a market cap of just under $1 billion.

The Russell 2000 is the most widely recognized index for small-cap stocks. Though the index contains smaller, more volatile companies, the Russell 2000 has handily outperformed its large-cap peers since

LARGEST COMPONENT COMPANIES				SECTOR COMPONENTS	
Company	Symbol	% of Index		Sector	% of Index
Tesoro Petro.	TSO	0.2%		Financial Services	21.4%
Calpine	CPN	0.2%		Industrial Materials	14.9%
Techne	TECH	0.2%		Healthcare	12.4%
Cytec Ind.	CYT	0.2%		Business Services	10.6%
Park National	PRK	0.2%		Hardware	9.9%
Energen	EGN	0.2%		Consumer Services	9.0%
Bancorpsouth	BXS	0.2%		Consumer Goods	5.3%
Idex Corp.	IEX	0.2%		Software	4.9%
Pediatrix Medical	PDX	0.2%		Energy	4.8%
Hyperion Solutions	HYSL	0.2%		Utilities	3.0%

If you wish to hide your character,
do not play golf.

— PERCEY BOOMER

its inception. It trades by far more shares than all of the other Russell ETFs put together.

The options for IWM are quite liquid as well, and there are some interesting aspects of the current option prices that makes it an excellent choice of an underlying for the *36% Solution*. As I write this (late 2006), the Implied Volatility (IV) for the IWM LEAPS (2008 and 2009) averages about 22% while the short-term options (October = 29%, November = 27%) have much higher IVs, creating a strong IV Advantage for this portfolio. It isn't necessary that there is an IV Advantage for the *36% Solution* to be successful, but it helps.

Volatility of the Russell 2000. Since we all know that volatility is the enemy of the *36% Solution*, it is important to take a peek at how much the stock has fluctuated each expiration month. I went back seven years with this study. See the table below.

EXPIRATION MONTH CHANGES IN PRICE OF RUSSELL 2000 (IWM)

	2001	2002	2003	2004	2005	2006	2007
January	6.6%	-2.4%	0.3%	8.4%	-4.6%	3.9%	-1.4%
February	2.0%	-0.6%	-7.7%	-1.7%	3.3%	3.5%	4.4%
March	-11.1%	6.5%	5.1%	-1.6%	-2.8%	2.0%	-4.8%
April	6.0%	3.7%	2.1%	2.4%	-4.8%	3.8%	6.5%
May	8.4%	-1.5%	8.8%	-6.4%	3.3%	-6.2%	-0.7%
June	-2.1%	-9.4%	7.6%	4.6%	5.6%	-4.2%	3.2%
July	-1.8%	-15.7%	3.3%	-2.7%	3.1%	-2.9%	-1.3%
August	-2.4%	2.2%	2.2%	-1.3%	-1.3%	6.3%	-5.8%
September	-20.1%	-7.1%	10.2%	5.0%	2.8%	2.4%	3.3%
October	12.2%	-1.0%	0.1%	-0.5%	-3.3%	4.0%	-2.3%
November	6.4%	6.1%	1.5%	7.9%	6.2%	4.0%	-3.5%
December	7.2%	0.8%	3.5%	4.2%	1.4%	0.4%	3.0%

It is a little hard to see strong seasonal patterns except that for six of the past seven years, November and December have been up months. August would probably have been the most profitable month because the percentage changes were all small except for 2006 and

1

*One thing about golf is you don't know
why you play bad and why you play good.*

— George Archer

2007. (Remember, the *36% Solution* makes money if the stock goes either up or down, just as long as the change is not a significant one. The *36% Solution* almost always makes a gain when the stock changes by less than 5% in an expiration month, as has been the case in three out of four months over the last five years.)

We should probably discount the huge drop in September 2001 but note that two months after the disaster, the stock was higher than it was the day before. Having a long time to recover from such events (by owning 2+ year LEAPS) is an important part of the *36% Solution* strategy.

It is clear that the market was less volatile between 2004 and 2006, and we know that it became more volatile in the second half of 2007 (except that the monthly percentage changes do not show it because price increases and decreases often cancelled one another out). All the double-digit price changes took place before September 2003 when option prices were considerably higher than they are today. Presumably, if the market becomes more volatile, option prices typically will rise as well, giving us more premium to work with and allowing us to make a profit even if the stock fluctuates more than it has historically.

Time is money.

— BENJAMIN FRANKLIN

Time is everything.

— NAPOLEON

I hate quotations.

— RALPH WALDO EMERSON

Appendix E
TERRY'S TIPS TRACK RECORD
AS OF DECEMBER 21, 2007

For the most current results, go to **www.TerrysTips.com/Track-Record**.

There are two variations of the basic strategy. The *Multiple Calendar Variation* uses calendar spreads (also called time spreads or horizontal spreads) at several different strike prices, some below and some above the current price of the stock. The *Diagonal Variation* has long positions at several strikes as well, but when new option positions are sold, they are predominantly the next-month option with the most time premium rather than selling the next-month option at the same strike prices as the long options.

36% Solution – Calls **Portfolio.** This portfolio was created in February 2007 with $10,000, using the *Russell 2000* (small cap ETF – IWM) as the underlying. It employed the *Diagonal Variation* of the *10K Strategy*, using Jan09 LEAPS as the long side. The annual goal of the portfolio is to earn 36% each year regardless of which way the market moves. Each month when there is a gain of 3%, $300 is withdrawn from the portfolio. If a gain of $600 or more is made (and the portfolio value is still above $10,000, $600 is removed). After 10 full expiration months, $5,400 had been withdrawn from the portfolio and the portfolio value was worth over $10,000. **Since its inception, the *36% Solution – Calls* portfolio has earned at a rate of 59% annualized, well above its target of 36%. It had gained 36% in the first 5½ months of operation.**

These results were achieved in spite of the fact that two weeks after the portfolio was established, IWM experienced the greatest weekly loss it had incurred in four years, and the stock dropped again by record amounts late in July. Since the portfolio was started, the Russell 2000 has fallen by over 7%. It is remarkable that a 59% annualized gain was achieved during this time period because the portfolio was designed to do best when the market went higher rather than lower.

137

36% Solution – Puts **Portfolio.** This portfolio was created in June 2007 with $10,000, using the *Russell 2000* (small cap ETF – IWM) as the underlying. It employs the same strategy as the *36% Solution – Calls* portfolio except that puts are used rather than calls. Put spreads are typically cheaper to place than same-strike call spreads, and the short-term time premium is about the same for puts and calls, so we expect that this portfolio might out-perform the same strategy using calls.

In its first 6 months in operation, this portfolio covered the bid-asked-spread-penalty of a new portfolio and gained slightly over 28% which works out to 59% on an annual basis. In similar fashion to the *36% Solution – Calls* portfolio, $3,600 was withdrawn from the port-folio, and it is still worth more than its starting $10,000.

36% Solution Big Bear **Portfolio.** This portfolio was created in August 2007 with $10,000, using the Russell 2000 (small cap ETF – IWM) as the underlying. It employs the same strategy as the 36% Solution – Puts portfolio except that a negative net delta position is retained at all times (i.e., it will be short). This portfolio is designed to do best when the market is weakest. It is a good addition for inves-tors who have other investments that do better in up markets.

In its first 10 weeks, the portfolio maintained a strongly short posi-tion so that it would prosper in a down market, and when the stock went up instead, the portfolio made an annualized gain of 55%. This was like having your cake and eating it too. In the third month when the underlying fell in value, the annualized gain soared to 119%. In the first 17 weeks of its existence, $3,600 was withdrawn from the portfolio and its value was still higher than the starting $10,000. At that time, its annualized gain was 94%.

10K Apple 3 **Portfolio.** This is one of our most aggressive portfo-lios, and uses the *Multiple Calendar Variation* of the *10K Strategy*. It was originally started in July 2005 with $10,000. By November 2005 it had doubled in value, and was started over as *Apple 2*, again with a starting value of $10,000. By May 2007, it had doubled in value for a second time, and was started over as *Apple 3* again with a starting value of $10,000. For investors in the original portfolio who did not remove cash when the portfolio had doubled in value, their initial $10,000 had grown to become four $10,000 "units" with a value of over $56,000 in less than two years. It is interesting to note that we traded almost exclusively with puts rather than calls in this portfolio even though the stock marched steadily higher throughout the period.

DIA Sleeping Giant **Portfolio.** This, one of our most "conservative" portfolios, was created in September 2004 with $20,000. The underlying is the Dow Jones Industrial Average tracking stock (DIA). It uses in-the-money call LEAPS for the long side, and the *Diagonal Variation* of the *10K Strategy*. The portfolio maintains a slightly bullish posture, and is designed to gain a relatively modest 20–30% a year in value. In its first two years, the portfolio had gained an average of 26% each year. After 2 years, $15,000 was withdrawn from the portfolio (leaving a balance of about $15,400), and just over a year later, the portfolio had grown to a value of $23,158, for a gain of 42% annualized.

Fifty & Out **Portfolio.** This portfolio uses the ETF Oil Services (OIH) as the underlying. It is designed to earn 50% a year, and is more "conservative" than two other Oil Services portfolios which use the same underlying. It employs the *Diagonal Variation* of the *10K Strategy*. The portfolio was started with $10,000 in February 2006 with the understanding that if and when the value reached $15,000, we would withdraw $5000. That milestone was achieved in May 2007. In November 2007, another $5,000 gain was registered, and it was withdrawn from the portfolio. At this point, original investors in this portfolio had all their money back and were playing entirely with profits.

10K Oil Services 4 – Calls **Portfolio.** This portfolio is a continuation of Oil Services 3 which doubled in value in 9 months and became Oil Services 4 in May 2007. The portfolio employs the *Diagonal Variation* of the *10K Strategy*. Oil Services 1 and Oil Services 2 each gained over 70% annualized before being replaced by Oil Services 3. The current portfolio has gained at the annualized rate of 71% since its inception in August 2006.

10K Oil Services 5 – Puts **Portfolio.** This portfolio was started in May 2007 with a starting value of $5,000. It uses the same strategy as *Oil Services 4 – Calls* except that puts are used instead of calls. We expect better returns using puts than calls, although only time will tell. While the portfolio was solidly ahead on the day before the October expiration, the stock fell over $12 on expiration Friday, and pushed the portfolio into the red. This is our only current portfolio that is now worth less than its starting value. At this time, the portfolio has lost slightly less than 10%.

Russell 1 **Portfolio.** This portfolio was created in September 2006 with $10,000. It was our first attempt to use the *10K Strategy's Multiple Calendar Variation* to achieve a moderate (36%) annual target with a high likelihood of achieving it. It was the beta version for the *36% Solution*. We tried (unsuccessfully, at first) several different methods of making this goal before finally settling on a new set of *Trading Rules* that have resulted in much improved results. The long side of our spreads now have only a few months of remaining life. While the results have improved with the new *Trading Rules* there have been far more fluctuations in portfolio value than is appropriate for a *36% Solution* portfolio, (which is supposed to enjoy slow, steady, reliable growth). This portfolio has experienced 10% monthly swings in value on several occasions. At this time, it has gained 60% since it started 15 months ago.

Russell 3 Portfolio. This portfolio was started in April 2007 to execute the newly-established *Trading Rules* for the *Russell 1* portfolio but with only $5,000 of starting value. Its value will rise or fall pretty much in tandem with the *Russell 1* portfolio. The portfolio is not yet 9 months old, and has gained over 50% in value since it was established.

Smiling Spider Portfolio. This is our newest portfolio, and is designed to be our most conservative. It uses the S&P 500 tracking stock, SPY, as the underlying, and the *Diagonal Variation* of the *10K Strategy*. True LEAPS are bought, and the portfolio consists of about equal numbers of puts and calls. In the first ten weeks of its existence, the portfolio covered the bid-asked-spread-penalty and chalked up a 10% gain, which works out to be about 50% annualized.

Discontinued Portfolios. In 2006 and 2007, ten portfolios were discontinued. Some were replaced by new portfolios using the same underlying. For example, *Oil Services 1* and *Oil Services 2* (both started with $10,000) were replaced by *Oil Services 3* with a starting value of $5,000 so more subscribers could mirror our trades.

Other portfolios were discontinued (usually at a loss) because the underlying stock or ETFs became too volatile compared to the option prices. One underlying (Phelps Dodge) was bought out by another company and ceased to exist. The buy-out premium was unusually large, Phelps Dodge shot up in price, and we suffered a $3,100 loss on our $5,000 starting portfolio value. It was a reminder of the potential danger of using a single company as the underlying rather than an ETF consisting of many companies (like DIA, IWM, SPY, and OIH that we use in other portfolios).

Bottom Line for Discontinued Portfolios. The 10 discontinued portfolios started with a composite value of $87,000. When they were discontinued, the composite value was $105,960, after paying all commissions. On average, these portfolios had been in existence about a year. If a subscriber had mirrored these portfolios (by himself or through Auto-Trade with his broker), he or she would have earned over 20% on his money (after commissions) for the year. Since most of our "failures" were included in this group, we think a 20% gain for a year isn't really so bad.

Earlier Year Results

The first year that *Terry's Tips* ran actual portfolios for subscribers to follow (and mirror if they wished) was 2003. Results were spectacular. Our QQQQ portfolio gained 196% for the calendar year. Our DIA portfolio gained 60% in value. 2004 was an entirely different story. A combination of 9-year-low option prices and a choppy market caused devastating losses in our QQQQ portfolios in 2004. This experience caused us to modify our strategy dramatically, and to select individual stocks or ETFs which had higher option prices and/or lower volatilities than QQQQ. We have concluded that unless option prices become considerably higher, our strategy does not work with QQQQ.

Results for 2005

In 2005, with our new Trading Rules in place, we enjoyed a big turn-around from our dismal results in 2004. The average annualized gain for all 8 portfolios for 2005 (after commissions) was 103%. Some of the underlying stocks went up dramatically (some so fast that our gains were actually diminished, as the *10K Strategy* likes a flat market best). One portfolio (Sears) saw its underlying fall from $144 to $115 in 4 months while the portfolio gained 50% in value. The stock then reversed direction and rose to $155 and the portfolio was up 108% after its first 10 months of existence.

We can't promise that we have created the perfect options strategy that achieves extraordinary gains in all kinds of markets, but we are quite proud of our performance for the past few years. We believe that our results have proved that the *10K Strategy* is just about the best possible investment strategy available to the individual investor.

Remember, options are leveraged securities, and are inherently more risky than conventional investments. Otherwise, the kinds of gains we have achieved in these years would not be possible.

You can check out the latest results of these portfolios at **www.TerrysTips.com/TrackRecord**.

I'd play every day if I could.
It's cheaper than a shrink and there
are no telephones on my golf cart.

— BRENT MUSBURGER

Index

A

Adjustment costs, 59
Adjustment Trading Rules, 71, 77, 81, 83
Allen, Debbie, 3, 5
Allen, Terry, 3, 28, 35
Amstrad electronics company, 32
Analyst(s), 27, 31
Annualized gain, 3
Antarctica, 125
Apple Computer, 65, 117, 138, 139
Archer, George, 134
Argentina, 79
Armour, Tommy, 21
Arnott, Robert, 9
At-the-money option, 50, 61, 71, 97
Auto-Trade, 89, 91, 93, 101, 105, 142
Average daily decay, 81,85,101

B

Balis, Tony, 12
Bancorpsouth, 131
Barber, Miller, 116
Bartokomous, Halki, 94
Beard, Henry, 122
Beckman, Martha, 112
Berkshire Hathaway, 19
Bid-Asked spread, 71
Bid-asked spread penalty, 67, 99, 123
Bishop, Jim, 60
Black-Scholes model, 35
Bogle, Jack, 11, 17, 19
Bolt, Tommy, 88
Boomer, Percey, 132
Break-even, 79, 83
Broker(s), 26, 27, 29, 71, 87, 89, 91, 93
Brokers, full-service, 27
Brooks, Mel, 102
Buffett, Warren, 9, 19, 20

Burlington Boys & Girls Club, 37
Buying stock(s), 13, 15, 21, 33

C

Calendar spread(s), 101, 111, 113, 117, 119, 121, 123, 137
Call (definition), 49
Call writing, 61,
Calpine, 131
Charities, 37
Cheating, 2
Chicago Board Options Exchange (CBOE), 35, 115
Commissions, 27, 49, 63, 127, 141, 142
Composite Market Timing Model, 97
Confessions of a Wall Street Analyst (Reingold), 12
Covered calls, 61, 63
Cytec Ind., 131

D

Daley, Arthur, 66
Decay, 55, 57
Delta, 109, 111, 113, 115, 138
Diagonal Variation, 69, 137, 139, 140, 141
Dickinson, Gardner, 118
Dillard Department Stores, 31
Diller, Phyllis, 50
Discount brokers, 49, 89, 91, 127
Dow Jones Industrial Average, 3
Dow Jones Industrial Average tracking stock (DIA), 129, 139, 141, 142
Downgrades, 31

E

Ellis, Charles, 17, 19, 21, 25
Emerson, Ralph Waldo, 136

Energen, 131

Excel software, 79. 101

Exercise of options, 125, 127, 129

Exchange Traded Fund (ETF), 13, 65, 67, 95, 97, 131, 132, 133, 137, 138, 139, 141, 142

Ex-dividend date, 125

Expiration Date, 49, 55, 77, 79, 81, 8.˙ 95, 101

Extraordinary Tennis for the Ordinary Tennis Player (Ramo), 21

F

Fannie Mae, 63

Flat markets, 9, 11

Floyd, Raymond, 100

Forbes, B. C., 22

Forbes magazine, 11, 22

Ford, Gerald, 126

Franklin, Benjamin, 136

Full-service broker(s), 27

G

Gallico, Paul, 110

Gamma, 109, 111, 113

Garden Notes from Muddy Creek (Allen), 3

General market trend, 97

Getty, J. Paul, 28

Golf, My Slice of Life (Ray), 5

Golfing (Beard), 122

Golf swing, 22, 44, 82

Golfer's Creed, 2

Google, 65, 113

Graphing software, 79

Graham, Benjamin, 20

Greeks, 109, 113, 115

Gulbenkian, Nubar, 124

H

Half, Robert, 40

Harrelson, Ken, 72

Harvard Business School, 35

Harvey, Paul, 108

Hebner, Mark T., 70

Historic volatility, 115

Hoffman, R. K., 122

Hogan, Ben, 44

Hope, Bob, 58

How to Play Your Best Golf All the Time (Armour), 21

Howard, M. S., 122

Hulbert, Mark, 11

Hutchinson, Horace G., 80

Hyperion Solutions, 131

I

Idex Corp., 131

Index fund, 19, 43

Implied Volatility, 109, 115, 133

Insurance, 59, 73, 75, 79

In-the-money option, 51, 69, 71, 81, 83, 99, 109, 111, 125, 129

Intrinsic value, 51, 127

Investment advisor, 5

IRA, 87, 89, 103, 107, 127, 129

J

John-Roger, 96

K

Karlgaard, Rich, 11

Kiyosaki, Robert, 16

K-Mart, 30

L

Las Vegas, 19

"Lazy Way" strategy, 103

LEAPS, 40, 69, 73, 127, 129, 133

Leverage, 53

Lewis, Joe E., 130

Life 101 (John-Rogers & McWilliams), 96

Lim, Paul J., 11

Long-term capital gains, 87

Luck, 8, 22

Lynch, Peter, 19
Lynd, Robert, 90

M

Mankiw, Greg, 19
Marrin, Dean, 52
McGraw-Hill, 25
McWilliams, Peter, 96
Mental aspects of golf, 18
Milne, A. A., 104
Moore, John H., 78
Morley, Christopher, 34
Morningstar, 17
Multiple calendar variation, 69, 137, 138, 140
Musburger, Brent, 144
Mutual funds, 15, 17, 18, 25, 41, 43, 53, 87

N

Napoleon, 136
NASDAQ 100 (QQQQ), 63, 142
Natural price, 97
Net delta value, 111, 113
Net gamma value, 113
No Cash, No Fear (Allen), 3
Nobel Prize, 19, 30
Northern Exposure: Aurora Borealis, 64

O

Odds, 21, 25, 59
Oil Services ETF (OIH), 67, 139, 141
Option exercise, 125, 127, 129
Option prices, 35, 109, 115, 117, 133, 135, 141, 142
Option software, 79
Option spreads, 57, 59, 79
Option trading, 1, 3, 27, 35, 37, 39, 41, 87, 89
Out-of-the-money option, 51, 53, 64, 81, 99, 111
Oxymoron. 98

P

Park National, 131
Pediatrix Medical, 131
Perfect Strangers (Bartokomous), 88
Phillips, Michael, 68
Premium, option (definition), 51
Put (definition), 51
Puts and calls, 49, 51, 68, 115, 119, 138, 141
Putting, 36

R

Ramo, Simon, 21
Ray, Ted, 5
Reingold, Dan, 12
Research Affiliates, 11
Return on investment (ROI), 99, 121
Rice, Grantland, 54
Rich Dad, Poor Dad (Kiyosaki), 16
Risk, 27, 38, 39, 41, 43, 45, 53, 73, 77, 79, 87, 95, 97, 109, 111, 113, 119, 143
Risk profile graph, 77, 79, 81, 83, 105, 119, 121
Rolling over, 81, 85, 99
Rosin, Charles, 64
Russell 1000, 131
Russell 2000 (IWM), 13, 41, 65, 67, 69, 97, 131, 133, 137, 138
Russell 3000, 65, 131

S

Samuelson, Paul, 30
Schwab, Charles R., 19
Scully, Frank, 74
Sears Holdings, 119
Self publishing, 5
Selling short, 31
Shanks — No Thanks (Hoffman), 122
Sharpe, William F., 19
Shaw, George Bernard, 86
Shoot Strategy, 15
Short-term capital gains, 87

Short-term options, 67, 69, 71, 75, 83, 87, 95, 97, 101, 111, 119, 133
Snead, Sam, 76
Spanish proverb, 48
Spreads, 59, 83, 97, 99
Standard & Poor 500 (S&P 500), 13, 17, 19, 65, 131, 141
Stock options (employee), 13
Strike price, 49, 51, 53, 55, 61, 63, 69, 71, 79, 81, 83, 85, 99, 113, 115, 119, 123, 127, 137
Sugar, Alan, 32

T

Taxation, 87
Teche, 131
10K Strategy, 63
Tennis, 21
Tennis for Beginners (Howard), 118
Terry@TerrysTips.com, 5
Terry's Tips (newsletter), 1, 5, 63, 75, 79, 87, 89, 91, 93, 95, 97, 101
Tesoro Petroleum, 131
The Only Investment Guide You Will Ever Need (Tobias), 26
The Producers (Brooks), 102
The World is Flat (Friedman), 9, 11
Theta, 109, 113, 115
Thinkorswim, 71, 89, 91, 93, 107, 115
36% Solution, 3, 21, 23, 28, 29, 41, 43, 57, 59, 63, 65, 67, 69, 77, 79, 81, 87, 89, 97, 99, 103, 105, 107, 111, 113, 117, 123, 127, 133, 135, 137, 138, 140
Time premium, 51, 125, 127, 137, 138
Time spread(s), 119, 137
Tobias, Andrew, 26
Toscano, Harry, 62
Trade Alert, 71, 89, 91, 93, 105

Trading options, 1, 3, 27, 35, 37, 39, 41, 87
Trading Rules, 71, 73, 79, 85, 95, 97, 140, 141, 142
Trevino, Lee, 116

U

Underlying stock, 43, 63, 6567, 83, 95, 97, 133, 137, 138, 139, 141, 142
University of Virginia, 35
Updike, John, 84

V

Value Line, 9
Vanguard, 11, 17
Vardon, Harry, 24
Vega, 109
Vermont, 37
Virginia, University of, 35
Volatility, 65, 67, 69, 95, 97, 109, 115, 133

W

Wall Street Journal, 19
Wal-Mart, 31
Watson, Tom, 106
Whisper numbers, 13
Wiley, John, 3
Winning the Loser's Game (Ellis), 17, 21, 25
Writing covered calls, 61, 63
www.CBOE.com, 115
www.GardenBooks.com, 3
www.humanity.org, 12
www.Kaininito.com, 79
www.TerrysTips.com, 1, 15, 37, 63, 69, 107
www.Terry'sTips.com/TrackRecord, 143
www.thinkorswim.com, 89